Dance Composition

AN INTERRELATED ARTS APPROACH

Library of Congress Cataloging-in-Publication Data

Pomer, Janice, 1955-
 Dance composition : an interrelated arts approach / Janice Pomer.
   p. cm.
 ISBN-13: 978-0-7360-6790-4 (soft cover)
 ISBN-10: 0-7360-6790-6 (soft cover)
 1. Dance--Study and teaching. 2. Dance--Production and direction--Study and teaching. 3. Choreography--Study and teaching. 4. Modern dance--Study and teaching. 5. Dance--Social aspects--Study and teaching. I. Title.
 GV1589.P67 2009
 792.8--dc22
                                        2008032110

ISBN-10: 0-7360-6790-6
ISBN-13: 978-0-7360-6790-4

Copyright © 2009 by Janice Pomer

All rights reserved. Except for use in a review, the reproduction or utilization of this work in any form or by any electronic, mechanical, or other means, now known or hereafter invented, including xerography, photocopying, and recording, and in any information storage and retrieval system, is forbidden without the written permission of the publisher.

The Web addresses cited in this text were current as of July 2008, unless otherwise noted.

The art images used as a part of the design and overall look for this book were created by Shelagh Keeley.

Acquisitions Editor: Judy Patterson Wright, PhD; **Developmental Editor:** Ragen E. Sanner; **Assistant Editor:** Anne Rumery; **Copyeditor:** Jan Feeney; **Proofreader:** Anne Meyer Byler; **Permission Manager:** Dalene Reeder; **Graphic Designer:** Nancy Rasmus; **Graphic Artist:** Dawn Sills; **Cover Designer:** Bob Reuther; **Cover photography/montage:** Michael Reinhart **Photo Production Manager:** Jason Allen; **Art Manager:** Kelly Hendren; **Associate Art Manager:** Alan L. Wilborn; **Illustrator:** Keri Evans; **Printer:** United Graphics

Printed in the United States of America   10 9 8 7 6 5 4 3 2 1

Human Kinetics
Web site: www.HumanKinetics.com

United States: Human Kinetics
P.O. Box 5076
Champaign, IL 61825-5076
800-747-4457
e-mail: humank@hkusa.com

Canada: Human Kinetics
475 Devonshire Road Unit 100
Windsor, ON N8Y 2L5
800-465-7301 (in Canada only)
e-mail: info@hkcanada.com

Europe: Human Kinetics
107 Bradford Road
Stanningley
Leeds LS28 6AT, United Kingdom
+44 (0) 113 255 5665
e-mail: hk@hkeurope.com

Australia: Human Kinetics
57A Price Avenue
Lower Mitcham, South Australia 5062
08 8372 0999
e-mail: info@hkaustralia.com

New Zealand: Human Kinetics
Division of Sports Distributors NZ Ltd.
P.O. Box 300 226 Albany
North Shore City
Auckland
0064 9 448 1207
e-mail: info@humankinetics.co.nz

Dance Composition

AN INTERRELATED ARTS APPROACH

Janice Pomer

Original music composed by Barry Prophet

Human Kinetics

CONTENTS

EXERCISE FINDER vi
PREFACE ix
ACKNOWLEDGMENTS xix

PART I Dance and the Visual Arts

CHAPTER 1 Shapes 3
Exercise 1.1   Traveling Patterns 5
Exercise 1.2   Symmetrical Motifs 11
Exercise 1.3   Mosaics 15
Exercise 1.4   Weaving and Unweaving Shapes 19
Exercise 1.5   Traditional Brush Painting 25
Exercise 1.6   Modern Painting Techniques 30
Artist Highlight Interview: Ana-Francisca de la Mora 34

CHAPTER 2 New Spaces 39
Exercise 2.1   Landmarks 41
Exercise 2.2   Dancing Shadows 46
Exercise 2.3   Conceptual Dance for Alternative Spaces 50

Culminating Exercise for Dance and the Visual Arts 53
Artist Highlight Interview: Lin Snelling 58

PART II Dance and Music

CHAPTER 3 Rhythm and Tempo 65
Exercise 3.1   Heartbeats and Drumbeats 67
Exercise 3.2   Clap Hands 71
Exercise 3.3   Variations on a Theme 76
Exercise 3.4   Playing With Time 82
Artist Highlight Interview: Parmela Attariwala 85

CHAPTER 4 Texture and Tone Color 89
Exercise 4.1   Textural Exploration 91
Exercise 4.2   Tonal Exploration 95
Exercise 4.3   Found Sound 98
Exercise 4.4   Turn Your Radio On 103

Culminating Exercise for Dance and Music 108
Artist Highlight Interview: Nejla Yatkin 111

PART III Dance and the Dramatic and Literary Arts

CHAPTER 5 Emotions and Character 117
Exercise 5.1 Emotional Exploration 118
Exercise 5.2 Character Discovery 123
Exercise 5.3 Clowning 128
Artist Highlight Interview: Denise Fujiwara 134

CHAPTER 6 Words, Thoughts, and Actions 139
Exercise 6.1 Alliterations 141
Exercise 6.2 Vowels and Syllabic Phrases 147
Exercise 6.3 Soliloquy 152
Exercise 6.4 Monologue 156
Exercise 6.5 Dialogue 160

Culminating Exercise for Dance and the Dramatic and Literary Arts 164
Artist Highlight Interview: Emerita Emerencia 169

GENERAL ARTS GLOSSARY 175
MUSIC GLOSSARY 177
GLOSSARY OF PARTICIPATING ARTISTS 179
ABOUT THE AUTHOR AND THE COMPOSER 181
MUSIC FINDER 184

EXERCISE FINDER

Number	Title	Page	Accompanying handouts available on companion Web site	Accompanying music tracks on music CD
CHAPTER 1 SHAPES				
1.1	Traveling Patterns	5	Student Journal 1.1	1, 2, and 3
1.2	Symmetrical Motifs	11	Student Journal 1.2	4 and 5
1.3	Mosaics	15	Student Journal 1.3	6
1.4	Weaving and Unweaving Shapes	19	Student Journal 1.4	7 and 20
1.5	Traditional Brush Painting	25	Student Journal 1.5	8
1.6	Modern Painting Techniques	30	Student Journal 1.6	9
CHAPTER 2 NEW SPACES				
2.1	Landmarks	41	Student Journal 2.1	Sonic needs will vary
2.2	Dancing Shadows	46	Student Journal 2.2	Any of the more atmospheric compositions, such as 5, 15, or 16
2.3	Conceptual Dance for Alternative Spaces	50	Student Journal 2.3	None
Culminating Exercise for Dance and the Visual Arts		53	• Self-Evaluation for Dance and the Visual Arts • Rubric for Culminating Exercise for Dance and the Visual Arts	Each dancer's choice
CHAPTER 3 RHYTHM AND TEMPO				
3.1	Heartbeats and Drumbeats	67	Student Journal 3.1	10
3.2	Clap Hands	71	Student Journal 3.2	11, 12, and 13
3.3	Variations on a Theme	76	Student Journal 3.3	12, 14, 15, and 16
3.4	Playing With Time	82	Student Journal 3.4	17, 18, and 19
CHAPTER 4 TEXTURE AND TONE COLOR				
4.1	Textural Exploration	91	Student Journal 4.1	20, 21, and 22
4.2	Tonal Exploration	95	Student Journal 4.2	23, 24, and 25
4.3	Found Sound	98	Student Journal 4.3	None
4.4	Turn Your Radio On	103	Student Journal 4.4	26
Culminating Exercise for Dance and Music		108	• Instructions on Creating Computer-Assisted Music • Self-Evaluation for Dance and Music • Rubric for Culminating Exercise for Dance and Music	35-72

Number	Title	Page	Accompanying handouts available on companion Web site	Accompanying music tracks on music CD
CHAPTER 5 EMOTIONS AND CHARACTERS				
5.1	Emotional Exploration	118	• Student Journal 5.1a • Student Journal 5.1b	27-33
5.2	Character Discovery	123	Student Journal 5.2	15, 16, or other atmospheric pieces
5.3	Clowning	128	Student Journal 5.3	14
CHAPTER 6 WORDS, THOUGHTS, AND ACTIONS				
6.1	Alliterations	141	Student Journal 6.1	None
6.2	Vowels and Syllabic Phrases	147	Student Journal 6.2	34
6.3	Soliloquy	152	Student Journal 6.3	Any atmospheric piece
6.4	Monologue	156	• Student Journal 6.4a • Student Journal 6.4b	None
6.5	Dialogue	160	Student Journal 6.5	None
Culminating Exercise for Dance and the Dramatic and Literary Arts		164	• Student Journal for Culminating Exercise for Dance and the Dramatic and Literary Arts • Self-Evaluation for Dance and the Dramatic and Literary Arts • Rubric for Culminating Exercise for Dance and the Dramatic and Literary Arts	None

> The real journey of discovery consists not in seeking new landscapes but in having new eyes.
>
> Marcel Proust

PREFACE

Dancers explore angular and curved shapes, negative and positive space, textures, rhythmic patterns, and shifting qualities and quantities of dramatic energy and emotion. These elements are first introduced in children's creative movement classes and continue to be developed in technique and composition classes. But these elements are important not just to dance; they are the building blocks for all of the arts and are part of the bond that dance shares with visual, musical, and dramatic and literary arts. By studying how artists working in other disciplines use these elements, dancers develop a more profound understanding of how to manipulate them in movement composition.

Dance by its very nature interacts with the other arts. Choreographers create visual, musical, and dramatic works to engage the viewers' eyes, ears, mind, body, and spirit. When they embody shapes and lines, rhythms and textures, narratives, poetry, and emotions, dancers become the art and the artist, the music and musician, the story and the storyteller. By recognizing and responding to the multidisciplinary nature of dance, performers and choreographers of all movement backgrounds can increase their performance dynamics and artistic sensibilities.

This book provides opportunities for exploring the interactive relationship between dance and the other arts. Each exercise is an artistic journey that encourages participants to experience movement in new ways. Working with architecture and examples of paintings and ceramics brings new insight to the body's use of shape, line, and space. Listening to percussive, microtonal, and environmental compositions brings new awareness of texture, timing, and harmonic relationships in dance. Vocalizing vowel sounds, syllabic phrases, and short pieces of text teaches internal narrative skills, emotional expression, and character development.

Dancers needn't study the evolution of Western art history in order to understand line and form. That information is beneficial and inspirational, but Western art history is not what the exercises in this book emphasize. And it's helpful, but certainly not imperative, for a dancer to know how to notate Western-based music scores. Lack of notation skills won't deter a dancer from developing musical dexterity and sonic sensitivities. Instead of focusing solely on classical Western art, music, and theater, these exercises examine traditional and contemporary art forms from around the world and explore ways of physically interpreting what is heard, seen, spoken, and emoted through movement experimentation.

About the Process

All of the exercises in this book encourage participants to observe aspects of other art forms and apply them to dance. It's a simple process of observation, exploration, creation, and reflection. The first step, observation, is constantly at play. Think of it as the common denominator (the bottom number of a fraction) which unites the other steps. Dance artists have been following this process since the earliest times. The first dances were created by those who

- observed the world around them;
- explored ways of imitating or symbolizing what they observed with their bodies;
- created dances to celebrate, commemorate, or communicate what they had observed; and
- reflected on and responded to the views of those who experienced the dance.

All of the exercises adhere to this template:

Observation: A concept is introduced.

Internal Exploration: Work independently.

External Exploration: Work with and observe others.

Group Reflection: Discuss observations from explorations.

Creation and Presentation: Apply information from exploration and reflection into a choreographic work.

Final Group Reflection: Discuss the choreography presented.

Student Journal: Record what you learned and ideas for future choreography.

The process isn't unique to dance or the arts. Scientists, architects, educators, and corporations employ this process in their think tanks and study groups. A problem is presented and studied by each member of the group. And because the think tank is purposely composed of individuals with various skills and backgrounds, every member brings a unique perspective to the problem-solving process. The same is true for each member of a composition class. Think tanks brainstorm; dance groups "bodystorm." Each person interprets an idea or movement differently. By observing, sharing, discussing, and comparing those differences, each member of the class becomes a wiser choreographer.

Bodystorming, like brainstorming, requires a generous nature. The internal and external explorations are improvisational. Every idea and interpretation is out there. Every impulse should be followed and explored. All of those inspirational elements, which have been witnessed by the class, are available for the whole class in their planned compositional works. As a result, the movement pieces created are collective compositions.

The collaborative aspect of compositional work isn't just physical; it's emphasized in all areas of the process. The structured group reflections highlight that. These discussions are a forum for expressing views. Sometimes people will

> *The question is not what you look at—but how you look and whether you see.*
>
> ~ Henry David Thoreau

speak on personal and internal experiences, other times on opinions formed while watching others work. Being articulate and constructive can be difficult, but it's a skill that artists in all disciplines need to develop. For example, while blocking a scene, an actor who was following script notes entered, walked to center stage, and stood beside a chair that had been placed there. The director said, "Don't stand beside the chair." So the actor sat down. Then the director said, "I didn't say sit on it." So the actor stood up, put the script on the chair, and replied, "I'm not good at guessing games. Why don't you just tell me what you'd like me to do?" Group discussions develop verbal skills. Be clear and concise, and give positive, concrete directions.

Journal Work

Journal entry handout sheets for recording personal observations are at the end of each exercise (available from the companion Web site). It's important to take time to record ideas and insights. An idea can appear and disappear in a heartbeat; journal entries help in recording and organizing those thoughts. You can use the journal after class to summarize the experience or during the week as a way of staying connected to the creative process. Written notes may be in point form or full sentences, and there's even space to draw.

Challenges Inherent in the Process

One of the challenges is to approach each exercise with new eyes—to not rely on choreographic tricks or physical technique, but to dig further and to discover new pathways of expression. At times it will be difficult, and as all explorers have realized, there will be times of frustration. It's all part of the process. When we explore new territory, we get lost—that's a reality. But the joy of discovery, whether in the arts, geography, or science, is palpable. Professor John Polyani, a Nobel-prize winner in physics, once said, "Scientists and artists keep the flame of creative thought alive." And just as mathematicians explore infinite possibilities with the numbers 0 to 9, choreographers explore the infinite visual, musical, and dramatic possibilities humans can communicate through movement.

Organization of the Book, CD, and Companion Web Site

The book is divided into three parts: one for visual arts, one for music, and one for literary and dramatic arts. The exercises in each part build from simplest to most challenging. At the end of each part is an in-depth choreographic project that uses the ideas and skills developed in the preceding exercises. This makes each part a complete entity. The book may be used over the course of three years (exploring a new section each year), or a class may use selected exercises from all of the parts in a one-year period. Much depends on the facilitator, course level, focus, and time constrictions.

Every class has its own character, and no two classes are alike. As a facilitator, you can work through the book from start to finish or select exercises you think will benefit students the most and explore those areas as deeply as you deem necessary. Spending four classes on one exercise can be as beneficial as completing an exercise each day. Developing movers with artistic sensibilities is the priority—use the exercises in the order that best suits students' needs.

Some of the interactive arts elements explored in one part are reexamined in another part. Each time an element is explored, it's from a unique perspective. For example, the exercises on space in part I explore how architectural spaces affect the way we move; exercises in part II explore how the space between silence and sound creates rhythm and harmony.

Part I: Dance and the Visual Arts

- Shape. Every line has shape, and every shape has line. Exploring an inside-and-outside approach to shape deepens physical and choreographic awareness. In dance we use the word *line* to describe anatomical line, line of focus or energy, or the dancer's pathway across the stage. In visual art, lines are pervasive—lines of color, texture, energy, and depth (opacity).
- Space. Part I looks at space architecturally, how the spaces we inhabit affect the way we move, and conceptually what dances we might create if we had no limitations.
- Light. Visual artists are virtuosos with light. They practice grayscales with lead pencils and charcoal, mix pigments to lighten and darken colors, layer paint to create luminosity, and "dodge and burn" photographs to intensify or brighten shadows. Here's a chance to explore light and shadow as a choreographic tool.

- Concepts and perspective. These are ideas beyond the concrete and choreography for the imagination.
- Culminating Exercise for Dance and the Visual Arts. This is an opportunity to create a solo inspired by a work of art.

Part II: Dance and Music
- Spatial relationships. The space between notes creates rhythms and harmonies. Explore the rhythmic potential within the body, develop listening skills, create and perform polyrhythmic movement structures, and learn to "see" rhythmic, melodic, and harmonic relationships.
- Time. Changes in tempo present choreographic and performance challenges.
- Pitch. In Western music terms, when a tuba and a flute play an A, the note is in a different pitch. In many world music traditions, notes are "bent" up or down from the pure tonic.
- Texture. Sounds can be manipulated to change textural quality. By bowing, strumming, and plucking a string instrument, you can produce a range of sonic dynamics.
- Tone color. Every instrument has a unique voice. The same note sung in the same pitch by two sopranos will have different tone colors. Without these musical elements, sound would be monochromatic. Pitch, texture, and tone color vibrate through every sound we hear (and those we don't), filling the air with complex sonic frequencies that influence how we move.
- Instrument making and found sound. Instruments are always evolving. It's believed that the first string instrument was a hunting bow—a weapon by day, an instrument by night. Discover how everyday items can be transformed into musical instruments and props for sonically rich and playful choreography.
- Composition. Create sonic compositions for dance using computer music software and a sample library of sounds.
- Culminating Exercise for Dance and Music. Compose music and choreograph a duet.

Part III: Dance and the Dramatic and Literary Arts
- Emotions. Actors use exercises to increase their emotional range just as dancers work daily to increase their physical range. The aim for both is to find the perfect balance between technical ability and emotional intensity.
- Character. One of the greatest challenges for writers and actors is to create believable characters as complex and multidimensional as real people. The observational skills actors hone are of great benefit to dancers looking for a deeper and richer performance experience.
- Clowning. Clowning is a form of physical theater combining elements of dramatic movement, dance, acting, storytelling, and political and social commentary. Clowns are masters of timing, gesture, and facial expression.

The clown, buffoon, fool, or trickster exists in all cultures; clowning is one of humanity's oldest performing art forms.
- Language. Writers select the words they use with the same compositional awareness as choreographers. The world of consonant and vowel sounds, syllabic phrases, individual words, and sentences is a rhythmic, sonic, emotional, and narrative resource for dancers.
- Culminating Exercise for Dance and the Dramatic and Literary Arts. Create an ensemble piece based on a folk tale.

Culminating Exercise

At the end of each of the three parts is a culminating exercise. These exercises incorporate the dance experiences explored in each section into longer choreographic works. The culminating exercises demonstrate how well the students understand and synthesize the material in each section. These exercises have their own assessment rubric addressing specific elements of the arts. But since the focus of the book is on experimentation and discovery, a different style of assessment is required for the experiential exercises. For the majority of the exercises, students can be assessed with the use of a general, process-based rubric (see the thumbnail of the General Rubric). This rubric supports and promotes self-discovery, self-discipline, self-motivation, and self-awareness. There are also student self-evaluation questions that can be completed at the end of each section.

Artist Highlight Interviews

It's great to have modern technological support, but dance is an ancient art form, and our most potent form of offering support

General Rubric

All handout materials are available on the companion Web site at www.HumanKinetics.com/DanceComposition.

has been an oral tradition with words of insight and inspiration passed down from teacher to student, from generation to generation. I tell stories my teachers told me, which are stories told to them by their teachers. I believe personal connections to be the most potent teaching tool. To highlight this tradition, I've interviewed several gifted artists who have graciously shared their time, experience, and personal insights with me so I might pass them on to you.

Arts Connections The Arts Connections are found at the end of every exercise. It's another way for students to extend their knowledge of other art forms and artists. Each Arts Connection has a paragraph or two introducing an artist or art form. At the end of each Arts Connection is a Web address for readers to refer to for further information.

Accompanying Music CD

Figure 1
This icon appears throughout the book alongside material related to the music CD as a reminder that the CD, which is bound into the back of the book, is available for use.

The music CD contains original compositions created for this text by composer, musician, instrument maker, and visual artist Barry Prophet. Many of the exercises rely on his music. At the top of each exercise the corresponding track numbers are clearly stated along with an icon to help point out the tracks (see figure 1). Just as the exercises encourage developing new eyes, the music encourages developing new ears. Those accustomed to popular and Western classical music may find many of Barry's compositions sonically challenging. The compositions create an environment for deep listening. This means listening not only with the ears but also with the body. (This concept is further explored in part II, Dance and Music.) All of the compositions are listed in the music finder on page 184. The music finder is a quick reference guide listing each track, its title, corresponding lessons, length of composition, and a description of the composition. Some exercises offer a choice of tracks (refer to the music finder to compare the selections at a glance), other exercises are performed in silence, and others require dancers to vocalize or generate their own music.

Barry Prophet has composed for dance and theater companies since 1979 and has worked with me for over 25 years in music and movement performance and education projects in Canada. For *Dance Composition: An Interrelated Arts Approach*, Barry created a selection of compositions that encompass rhythmic percussion, world music, minimalist soundscapes, and textural atmospheres. Barry designed the computer-assisted music manual to guide students through the music software used in the culminating exercise in part II and created the sound library in the CD specifically for that project.

Companion Web Site

Thanks to new technologies, *Dance Composition: An Interrelated Arts Approach* is more than a textbook showing small black-and-white images. Looking at small black-and-white photographs of full-color art can be frustrating. To address this problem, the companion Web site offers a fuller learning experience. The Web site contains the following features:

- Color photographs of the artwork from part I are available for viewing on the Web site.
- Student journal pages present questions for personal reflection (the final step of the process for each exercise).
- Self-evaluation sheets provide a format for periodic assessment.
- General rubric sheets can be used throughout the text as the facilitator sees fit. There are specific rubrics for each of the culminating exercises at the end of chapters 2, 4, and 6.
- A manual on the use of computer-assisted music as required for the final exercise of part II walks students through the software used to create their own music.

Teacher as Facilitator

While working on the exercises in this book, the teacher will take on the role of facilitator. That job involves creating a dance laboratory environment where dance students develop artistic awareness and personal aesthetics through structured movement experiments. Students shouldn't worry about performing the perfect pirouette or pleading contraction; the focus is on expressing emotions and experiencing movement in new and unusual ways.

The facilitator's most important function in this process is to create an environment where class members feel comfortable in these areas:

- Taking risks (physical and artistic)
- Being watched and watching others while improvising (bodystorming)
- Presenting works in progress to peers
- Expressing views in discussion
- Listening to others' views

These are the facilitator's other roles:

- Select exercises to be explored and sometimes assign groupings.
- Watch the work as it unfolds.
- Make sure everyone stays on task.
- Offer insights and observations in the discussion periods.

No one should be asked to explore and create in an environment where they feel repressed and constantly judged, but participating in a creative class completely lacking in structure or values can be equally frustrating. The exercises in this book help teachers and students find that balance through these clearly stated elements:

- Observation and exploration ideas
- Choreographic structures for students to interpret
- Questions to stimulate discussions, ensuring everyone has an equal opportunity to voice opinions in a constructive manner

The exercises strike a balance between exploration and dance creation. The time allotments for many of the exercises are short; they encourage students to experience a palette of stimuli and to quickly respond.

At any time the facilitator may lengthen the suggested times to allow students to focus on a specific area or skill. It's important to let your facilitator know when *you* are drawn to a particular exercise or concept—you may receive special permission to develop it further on your own time, or the time allotment for that exercise may be adjusted for the entire class.

It's a Personal Journey

Imagine a traveler walking up a mountain by way of an ascending spiral path. To reach the summit, he has to circle the mountain countless times. Around and around, each revolution takes him incrementally higher. When he looks out at the landscape, his view is forever changing. As he climbs higher and higher up the path, the tree trunks and branches become treetops, the treetops spread out into a forest, and he sees the rivers and lands that exist beyond the forest.

Continue with the image of the spiraling path and imagine each direction embodying one of the four steps in this book's creative template:

- North is observation.
- East is exploration.
- South is creation.
- West is reflection and response.

Every completion of a loop in the spiral returns the traveler to where he first began, only a little higher up along the path. What he saw on his previous circuit informs how he views the landscape the next time around. This is the artist's journey—and it doesn't stop at the summit.

The journey of discovery is never ending. Traveling down the spiraling path is as exciting as going up. Perspectives keep changing, the knowledge base grows, and it becomes second nature to observe, explore, create, and reflect every step along the path.

As the traveler descends, the sky, distant lands, and rivers disappear from view and the forest shifts into a thick green blur of leaves, but the knowledge of the sky and treetops remains. And at the bottom of the path the traveler sees pebbles, soil, moss, and roots on the forest floor and realizes that the forest floor is connected to everything he has seen on his journey to the top of the summit and back. They are the foundation supporting the trees in their quest to touch the clouds, linked to the rivers and the lands beyond the forest; they are the pillars on which the mountain rests.

The pebbles, soil, moss, and roots are akin to our elements of dance. By studying how artists work with line, musicians work with rhythm, and actors work with emotions, you'll view these dance elements from new perspectives and gain greater choreographic insight and ability.

ACKNOWLEDGMENTS

This book could not have been created without the generosity of photographers Adam Auer, Antonio Gómez-Palacio, David Hou, Diana Kolpak, John Lauener, Avril Patrick, David Powell, Barry Prophet, Michael Reinhart, Astrid Rieken, and Stefan Rose, and visual artist Shelagh Keeley. Their images grace the pages and add so much to the beauty of the book. Nor could the book have been written without the participation of Parmela Attariwala, Emerita Emerencia, Denise Fujiwara, Ana Francisca de la Mora, Lin Snelling, and Nejla Yatkin who took time out of their busy schedules to be interviewed for the artist highlights. Their collective knowledge and experience is inspiring.

Others who helped include Vivine Scarlett at dance Immersion, and Judy Wright Patterson, Ragen Sanner, and all the staff at Human Kinetics.

To Barry Prophet—whose music compositions enliven the exercises in the book just as his love enlivens everyday of my life—thank you.

The creative excellence and generosity of all of these contributors has made working on this text a most memorable journey.

PART I

Dance and the Visual Arts

When we decorate ourselves or our homes, we apply personal aesthetics to create a visual effect. Human beings have been creating functional and decorative designs since the earliest times. We create wearable art for our bodies, two-dimensional art for the walls of our dwellings, and three-dimensional art for the spaces we inhabit. Traditionally our environments have provided us with resources, and each culture developed technologies for carving wood and stone masks and sculptures, weaving organic and animal fibers into clothing and baskets, and crafting metal into jewelry, tools, and weapons.

Nejla Yatkin.
Astrid Riecken/The Washington Times.

Here's a list of the visual art forms to keep in mind while working on the exercises in part I.

Architecture, and all of the arts connected with buildings (stained glass, mosaic tiling, masonry)

Ceramics (decorative and utilitarian including tiles, beads, vases, bowls)

Drawing (pencil, charcoal, ink)

Jewelry (wearable art of metals, stones, shells, beads, feathers)

Painting (watercolor, oil, acrylic; on paper, canvas, caves, buildings, outdoor murals)

Photography, film, and video (live, animation, computer generated)

Print making (monoprints, screenprinting, wood blocks, and engraving)

Sculpture (marble and other stones, wood, metal, clay, fabric)

Textiles (weaving, batik, knitting, embroidery, tapestry)

Choreographers and visual artists manipulate many of the same elements: shapes, lines, weight of attack, spatial relationships, patterns, lighting, and perspective. Dance and visual art can be abstract or representational; it can be intimate or colossal. Both art forms embrace a wealth of practitioners working in a myriad of techniques, each requiring unique skills and aesthetic awareness.

In part I you'll explore visual elements that are applicable to dance and to two- and three-dimensional visual arts disciplines. Those elements include the following:

Line: curves and angles in border patterns, painting, and calligraphy

Shapes: symmetry, geometric motifs, negative and positive space

Deconstruction and abstraction: what you see and what you don't see

New spaces: architectural elements

Light: shadows, shading, shaping space with light

Concepts: formulating ideas

Perspective: personal interpretation

Note to Facilitator

Return for a moment to the image of the spiraling path up the mountain. The traveler finds that the first circuits up the mountain are the easiest: The slope is gentle and the landscape familiar.

The exercises in chapter 1 are similar. They explore familiar elements and the assignments are relatively simple. As the preface explains, these initial exercises are designed to sensitize students' responses to visual stimuli and mold the class into an artistic collective.

CHAPTER 1
Shapes

Dance is visual and visceral. A dancer need not have the ability to see, but audience members experience dance first through the eyes, then through the other senses and thought processes. The dancers' movement patterns, shapes, lines, and spatial relationships elicit emotional and intellectual responses in the viewers. It's the same experience as when we view visual art, whether it's a painting or sculpture, fabric or ceramic, figurative, architectural, or conceptual.

When we begin studying choreography, we're encouraged to observe the movement patterns around us, including patterns in nature and in our homes and work environment. Observing movement trains our eyes. While working on the exercises in chapters 1 and 2, apply those observation skills to the visual art around you. Functional or decorative, commercial or cultural, visual art is everywhere—in building facades, book covers, posters, and clothing. They're all conceived, designed, and constructed to be viewed.

Human beings make things. Visit a museum and you can't help but be amazed by the functional and decorative art created by early humans. You'll notice how every culture found unique ways to manipulate two basic shapes: the curve and the angle. Out of clay, wood, and metal, we fashioned pots, bowls, jugs, and cups. The same materials were used for spears, axes, arrows, and knives. The shape of cooking utensils hasn't changed much over the millennia, nor have the shapes of some weapons. You can still see the shape of an arrow in a

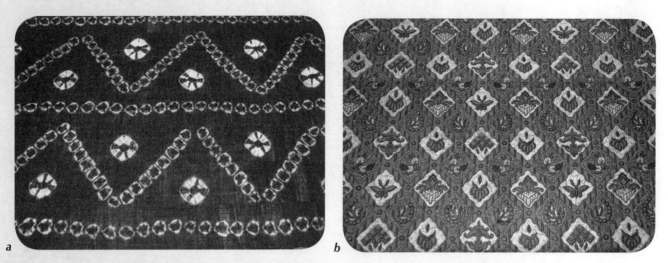

(a) An example of traditional African textile and (b) an example of traditional Indonesian textile. Both fabric designs feature a rounded diamond shape but employ contrasting use of space, direction, repetition, and ornamentation.
Barry Prophet, photographer. www.pomer-prophet.com.

supersonic jet—both shapes are aerodynamic. And the shape of a bowl is the shape of a wheel, one of the most essential devices used by humans. The circle is one of the great building blocks of humanity.

The shape of an object or an animal can dictate how it moves best. Snakes slither, hawks soar, kangaroos hop, and caterpillars creep. Whether it's assuming the shape of a technical dance position or simply manipulating the body, dancers are constantly confronted with the challenge of creating and embodying shapes. That challenge never ends; it moves from being purely physical to being one of depth and artistic awareness. Shapes have substance, and dancers need to connect with the energy of a shape to intensify the performance experience because shapes are more than physical. Written words are two-dimensional shapes. The shapes we make with our mouths when we speak are three-dimensional. The sounds we make when we speak or sing are shapes as well. We can feel and hear the sonic vibration rise and fall. Sounds have shapes and emotions do, too. Like sound, emotions can swell and recede. Emotions can surround you, and they can pierce you. Emotions are curved and angular, like bowls and arrows, wheels and walking sticks. We make shapes with the corporeal body, but as performers and viewers we experience shapes on a myriad of levels.

Exercise 1.1 Traveling Patterns

Translating Traditional Border Patterns Into Movement

This exercise uses border patterns from traditional ceramics, jewelry, and fabric as inspiration for creating traveling combinations.

Observation

MUSIC SELECTION
Tracks 1, 2, and 3

Lines have shape. If a line isn't perfectly straight, it's curved or angular. When two straight lines intersect, they create an angle. A single line can be used in delineating the finished edge on a piece of fabric or run along the circumference of a bowl, but more decorative border patterns are composed of curved and angular lines. Look at the images in figure 1.1. Do the angles and curves convey movement? Do they have a sense of direction? Do the shapes travel in distinct ways, as the arrow and the wheel do?

a

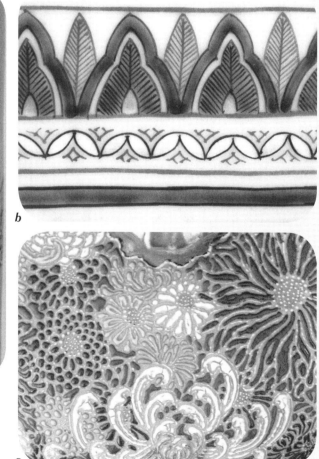

b

c

Figure 1.1
Examples of patterns in Asian art containing angles and curves, (a) carved in ivory and (b-c) painted on ceramics.

Barry Prophet, photographer. www.pomer-prophet.com.

Internal Exploration

MUSIC SELECTION
Tracks 1 and 2

Use track 1 to explore curved, circular, and spiraling shapes and traveling movements, then track 2 to explore angular, pointed shapes and traveling patterns. It's a simple exploration that warms up the body and mind. Have fun, be playful, try not to repeat, keep moving, and keep discovering.

1. Start in parallel, or neutral, position (shoulders over hips, hips over knees, knees over feet, feet hip-width apart, toes forward).
2. When the music begins (track 1), curve, wiggle, weave, and twist on the spot and travel throughout the room. Over the course of the music, be sure that you use every part of the body to explore curves.
3. Repeat the process, this time exploring angles. Start standing in parallel position; when the music begins (track 2), find as many ways as possible to be angular.

External Exploration

Apply the movement vocabulary from the internal exploration to an external exploration focusing on angular shapes in the air and curved shapes on the floor.

Line up one behind the other in three or four straight lines at one end of the room, as you would do in a technique class. The structure isn't meant to impose conformity; it's simply the safest way to use the space when several people are running and leaping at the same time. It also provides those not moving with a good view of those who are.

Variation 1: Curves

MUSIC SELECTION
Track 3 or silence if you prefer a different tempo

After 4 beats of introductory music (or call out 4 if working in silence), the first person in each line performs a variation on the following:

- Do a forward traveling movement of your choice for 2 to 6 beats.
- Freeze in a curved shape.
- Increase (deepen) the curve (such as rounding the spine, arms, or hands) for a minimum of 4 beats.
- Release it and move forward for 2 to 6 beats.
- Freeze in a different curved shape and deepen it for several more beats for a minimum of 4 beats.
- Release the shape and continue to the far side of the room.

Though the first person in each line starts at the same time, they probably won't finish at the same time. Wait until everyone is finished before the next group begins. Repeat that sequence at least two times, each time employing different circular shapes and move–freeze relationships.

Variation 2: Angles

After 4 beats of introductory music (or count 4 out loud if working in silence), the first person in each line performs the following:

Shapes

MUSIC SELECTION
Track 3 or silence if you prefer a different tempo

- Run forward (or other quick traveling step).
- Create an angular shape in the air.
- Land and run (or other quick traveling step).
- Create another angular shape in the air.
- Continue running to the far side of the room.

Repeat the sequence at least two times, each time employing different traveling patterns and angular airborne shapes.

Variation 3: Angles and Curves

MUSIC SELECTION
Track 3 or silence if you prefer a different tempo

1. After 4 beats of introductory music (or count 4 out loud if working in silence), the first person in each line performs the following:
   - Run forward (or other quick traveling step).
   - Create an angular shape in the air.
   - Land and travel forward.
   - Freeze in a curved shape.
   - Increase (tighten) the curve.
   - Move (roll, ripple, spin) to the end of the room while maintaining the integrity of the curved shape.
2. Repeat this sequence across the floor twice, each time exploring new relationships. Change the timing, the angular shape, and the curved shape; find new ways of traveling in the curved shape.

Safety Note

While performing, use peripheral vision and avoid interfering with others' movements.

Group Reflection

All of the traveling patterns moved forward, but the curves and angles added inward and outward direction and dynamics.

- Did the internal exploration prepare you for the external exploration? If yes, explain how.
- Did you employ emotional energy or performance dynamics to animate the contrasting shapes? If yes, explain how.
- Did you feel yourself or others become an arrow or a wheel?
- Which traveling combinations were the most eye catching? Identify who performed each one, and discuss the elements that made the combination exceptional.

Creation and Presentation

The line drawings in figure 1.2 are examples of patterns used in traditional ceramics, textiles, and jewelry from around the world. The first two designs can be translated into basic traveling steps by employing simple side, front, side, back footwork. For pattern *a*, the footwork could move in straight lines creating right angles with each direction change. To translate pattern *b*, the footwork could follow a curved or scalloped line. As a class, try translating patterns *a* and *b* and see how many variations you can come up with. (It's interesting to notice that even though pattern *b* uses curved lines, an angle appears at the frontmost and backmost connections to form points.)

Work in pairs and translate one of the more complicated patterns. Work in silence and explore internal rhythmic patterns to help highlight the angles and curves.

- Look at border patterns *c, d, e,* and *f*. Each has unique qualities that translate into movement through creative use of line, shape, spatial relationships, timing, levels, and energy.
- Select a pattern and create a traveling sequence inspired by that border design.
- Just because the patterns are flat doesn't mean the movement pattern should be. Leap, kick, wiggle, and roll. Apply physical and emotional experiences from the previous explorations.
- Take 5 to 10 minutes to work, then sit down in the audience area. One by one, each pair will present their work.
- Before presenting, always announce the border pattern being interpreted.

Final Group Reflection

Use the following questions to initiate a class dialogue.

- Was one pattern a more popular choice than the others? If yes, identify which pattern it was and ask those who selected it to explain why it was more appealing than the others.
- Was one pattern the least popular? If yes, discuss why. (Was it too difficult or uninteresting?) Get everyone's opinion if there was a pattern that no one used and, time permitting, have everyone translate it into movement. Were the results surprising? Did the pattern turn out to be more interesting or less difficult than originally thought?

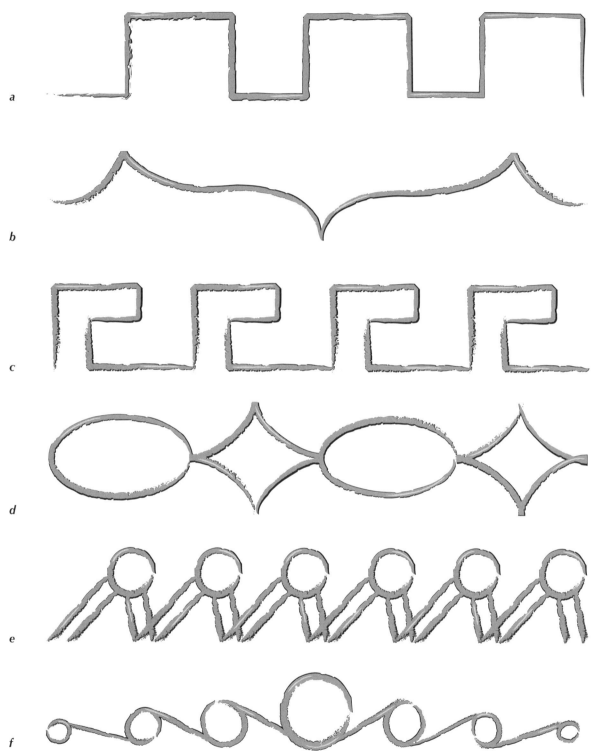

Figure 1.2
Border patterns.

Student Journal 1.1

All handout materials are available on the companion Web site at www.HumanKinetics.com/DanceComposition.

Arts Connections

One of Picasso's most famous paintings is his 1906-07 masterpiece *Les Demoiselles d'Avignon*. The painting is of five women and a still life. The figures are all angles and curves—three of the women are angular explorations of the classical style, whereas the other two figures have been influenced by traditional art from Africa and Polynesia. At first sight, the painting appears jarring and somewhat disconnected, but it's a fantastic blend of concave and convex angles and curves that create depth and motion. It's believed that an art critic first used the term *cubism* in response to this work because of the powerful use of angles and sharp edges. *Les Demoiselles d'Avignon* is at the Museum of Modern Art (MoMA) in New York. To see the painting online, go to www.moma.org/collection/conservation/demoiselles; to visit MoMA's main page, go to www.moma.org.

Border patterns haven't changed much over the centuries. Look at contemporary jewelry, ceramics, and textiles and compare them to centuries-old traditional patterns. Some things have changed, such as man-made materials and production techniques, but much has stayed the same. A good resource for viewing traditional and contemporary fabric art is the Textile Museum of Canada Web site at www.textilemuseum.ca. Also check out the Gardiner Museum site at www.gardinermuseum.on.ca to view traditional and contemporary ceramics from around the world.

Exercise 1.2 Symmetrical Motifs

Exploring Symmetrical Movement

MUSIC SELECTION
Tracks 4 and 5

This exercise explores ways of using symmetrical shapes beyond basic compositional positioning. We often choreograph using symmetrical spacing, creating a balanced stage by spacing an equal number of dancers on stage left and on stage right or by using mirror imaging in duets. Symmetrical patterns in visual art can be simple or intricate. The images in figure 1.3 are examples of traditional symmetrical patterns in visual art. Each of them communicates a sense of being complete and whole unto itself. The same is true for the circle of dancers in figure 1.4.

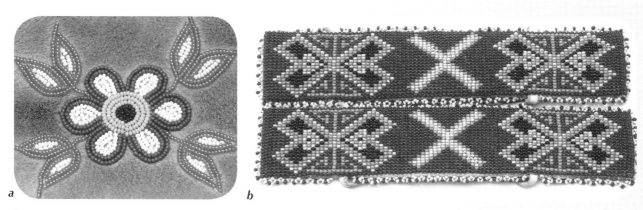

Figure 1.3
Six Nations symmetrical beadwork patterns, *a)* moose hide pouch and *b)* ornamental braid ties.
Barry Prophet, photographer. www.pomer-prophet.com.

Observation

Externally the human body is symmetrical; can it move that way, too? How much time does a person spend moving symmetrically? Can we be like the symmetrical images, complete unto ourselves? Imagine existing in a world where every action is symmetrical. We wouldn't be able to do some of the most basic things, such as walking. Walking requires moving one leg in front of the other. So how would we move?

Internal Exploration

MUSIC SELECTION
Track 4

Explore ways of moving through space while maintaining symmetry throughout.

1. Stand, lie down, or crouch in a symmetrical position.
2. When the music begins, explore symmetrical movement in all levels and dynamics. Travel across the floor, move up and down, and work large and small isolations.
3. Continue moving until the music stops, then freeze.

Figure 1.4
Dancers in a symmetrical circle.
Barry Prophet, photographer.
www.pomer-prophet.com.

External Exploration

Get into two groups. One group will perform the exercise while the other group watches. Then reverse roles. After everyone has had the opportunity to observe the exercise, discuss.

Group Reflection

Everyone should contribute to the conversation by answering the first question.

- Did you get stuck in a position thinking there's no hope of moving out of it in a symmetrical fashion? What was the shape and how did you solve the problem?
- Identify internal strengths you discovered while moving.
- How does the limitation of moving symmetrically increase some actions' dynamic and dramatic potential?

Creation and Presentation

This exercise of symmetrical duets requires three steps of structured exploration. The duets are most successful if partners are similar in size.

Preparation Step 1

MUSIC SELECTION
Silence

1. Take 3 to 4 minutes to create five symmetrically connected shapes. Partners may connect back to back, top of head to top of head, or soles of feet to soles of feet. Use multiple connections, such as elbows and knees or hands and shoulders, but connections you use for one shape shouldn't be repeated in any of the others.

2. Use a variety of levels, and don't forget to animate body parts other than those used in the connections to embellish the shape (such as extended legs and arms, flat back, flexed hands and feet).
3. Memorize each shape and assign an order to the shapes. Know which is shape 1, 2, 3, 4, and 5.

Preparation Step 2

MUSIC SELECTION
Track 5

1. Explore moving through the connected shapes using only symmetrical movement. Work slowly and smoothly. Imagine being an amoeba, a cell dividing itself into two equal parts.
2. On the sound of the first gong, move symmetrically into the first connected symmetrical shape. On the second gong, slowly move symmetrically from the first shape to the second. There should be no leader; watch and feel each other's impulses, especially if working "blind" with no visual contact. This requires concentration and sensitivity. Move with united intent and keep movements symmetrical throughout the entire exercise. Use very gentle pushing and pulling to signal each other. Use peripheral vision. Avoid sudden or erratic moves. Work slowly while moving through the five shapes.

You may find that you're working faster or slower than the gong. This exercise isn't about being "right"; it's about experiencing shapes and movement potential. Moving into and out of some shapes can be very complex and time consuming—some pairs won't be able to complete all five shapes by the end of the music. This step is experimental; its value is in bringing knowledge and inspiration to the upcoming choreographic assignment.

Preparation Step 3

MUSIC SELECTION
Track 5

Step 3 is purely experiential. The gong music is 1:40 minutes; it will be played three times, long enough to explore ways to animate the five connected shapes in the following manner:

- Travel across the floor without breaking the symmetry.
- Move up and down or from side to side without breaking the symmetry.
- Explore a variety of tempos and dynamics other than slow and sustained.

Unlike the work in solo symmetry, pairings can employ opposition work (setting one leg in front of the other) as long as it's in a symmetrical relationship.

Choreographic Requirements

MUSIC SELECTION
Track 4

Create a duet containing the following elements:

- Travel from offstage to center stage in an attached symmetrical shape.
- Work symmetrically to slowly transform into a second symmetrical shape.
- Separate and move into two different symmetrical shapes.
- Maintain individual symmetry while moving apart (partners will work with different symmetrical movements and shapes).
- Finish anywhere on stage in frozen solo symmetrical positions.

When everyone has completed the choreographic assignment, come together and present one duet at a time.

Final Group Reflection

- Was element 3 (separate into two different symmetrical shapes) a critical moment in the choreography? (Identify the most successful transitions and explain why they were so effective.)
- Did the choreography communicate a subtext (magnetic pulling, emotional attachment)? Identify and describe the duets in which the subtext was most apparent.

Arts Connection

The ancient Greeks, Cretans, and Romans used mosaics to decorate their homes and temples. In the sixth century AD, Byzantine artists began designing intricate mosaics for their churches by using small pieces of glass, semiprecious stones, and marble. During the Middle Ages, Islamic artists working throughout the Middle East and Spain perfected mosaic art by using symmetrically shaped ceramic tiles to create geometric and floral patterns of extraordinary beauty and complexity. Go to www.thejoyofshards.co.uk/history/index.shtml to view examples of ancient, classical, and modern mosaics.

Student Journal 1.2

All handout materials are available on the companion Web site at www.HumanKinetics.com/DanceComposition.

Exercise 1.3 Mosaics

MUSIC SELECTION
Track 6

Connecting Shapes

The exercise explores ways of connecting similar and contrasting shapes to create patterns and complex group shapes.

Observation

Look at figure 1.5, illustrations of traditional geometric tile patterns. The tinted tile shapes create the patterns within the patterns. Use the blank graphed squares in Student Journal 1.3 to explore repeated shapes (arrows, diamonds, circles, and so on). Figure 1.5, a through c, shows the evolution of a pattern containing square and octagonal tile pieces while figure 1.5, d through e, shows variations with small square tiles.

Internal Exploration

MUSIC SELECTION
Track 6

1. Work with a partner. Without talking, make an asymmetrical physical connection not involving the hands (such as head to hip, elbow to knee).
2. When the music comes on, find ways of moving as one without breaking the connection.
3. At random intervals, the facilitator will call out, "Change!" Without talking, quickly find a new asymmetrical connection and begin to move.
4. Make at least four changes before the exploration is complete.

External Exploration

MUSIC SELECTION
Track 6

Repeat the exercise with three or four pairs presenting while the others watch. Have every pair explore four different connections before moving on to the next group.

Group Reflection

- Exercise 1.2 explored symmetrical connections; this exercise looks at asymmetrical ones. Survey the class to see if one type of connection is preferred over the other, and if so, why? (Does a particular type of connection offer greater dynamics, mobility, or cohesion?)
- Identify the most physically challenging connections from this exploration. (Allow everyone time to try the connection and figure out ways of moving.) Discuss strategies for animating them.

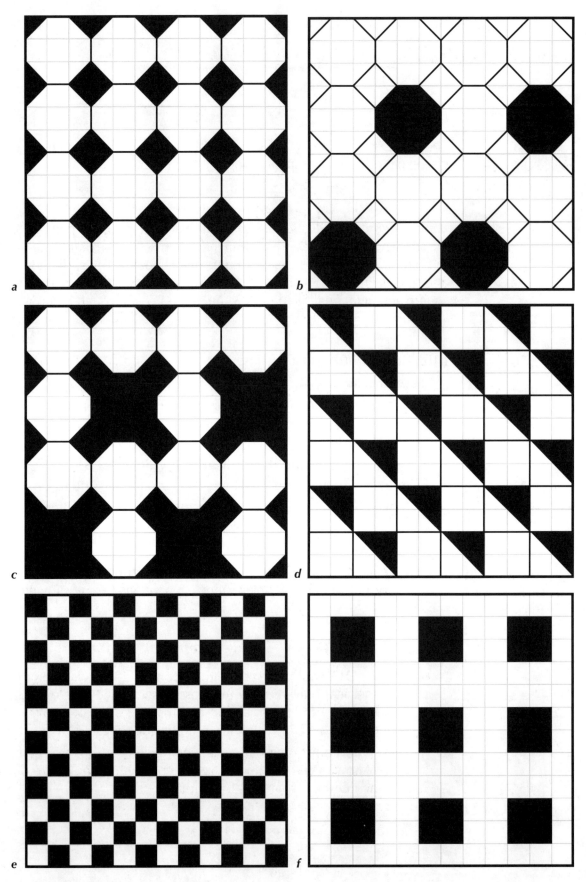

Figure 1.5
Traditional geometric tile patterns.

Box with mother-of-pearl mosaic inlay.
Barry Prophet, photographer. www.pomer-prophet.com.

Creation and Presentation

Work without musical accompaniment in groups of four or five and create an ensemble piece containing these elements:

- Everyone is connected using the same shape, connected in the same way (without using hands), and moving in at least two different ways.
- Everyone is connected using contrasting shapes (without using hands) and moving in at least two different ways.
- Individual dancers perform short, contrasting movement sequences.
- Use a canon sequence, or round. (See the music glossary on page 177.) The sequence requires no direct physical connections to other dancers.

After 30 minutes, ensembles will present and then discuss their work.

Final Group Reflection

- Compare all of the connected shapes and the ways in which they moved. Discuss each shape's dynamic and dramatic strengths.
- Was the space between bodies as important as the combined shape?
- How important were the individual and canon movement sequences to the form of the piece? (For example, did the canon sequence unite dancers without imposing a direct physical connection?)

Student Journal 1.3

All handout materials are available on the companion Web site at www.HumanKinetics.com/DanceComposition.

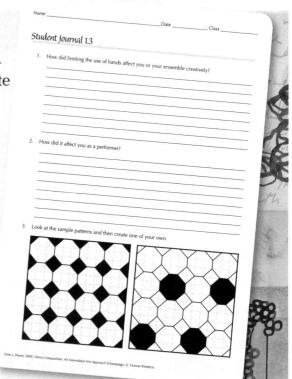

Exercise 1.4 Weaving and Unweaving Shapes

Playing With Shapes and Internal and External Space

MUSIC SELECTION
Tracks 7 and 20

This exercise combines experiences from the first three exercises in this chapter into an extended choreographic project for quartet, duet, and soloist.

Observation

Figure 1.6 is a hand-woven basket from South Africa containing a combination of angles and curves. The basket is infused with energy—lightning bolts cut inward from the outside edges and transform into a swirling whirlpool in the center. The foreground and the background vibrate against each other in symmetrical harmony. (When viewed on the Web site, the orange and red angles and curves pulse against the black. The colors aren't from traditional dyes; the basket was woven out of shiny plastic-covered copper telephone wires. It's an example of how even traditional art is never truly static. In this case, the artist combined ancient weaving techniques with 21st-century materials.)

Figure 1.6
African basket.
Barry Prophet, photographer.
www.pomer-prophet.com.

The pattern woven into the basket is composed of angles and curves. You explored outward manifestations of angles and curves in exercise 1.1, Traveling Patterns. This exploration highlights inner dynamics.

Internal Exploration of Angles

MUSIC SELECTION
Track 20

Stand in neutral position with your eyes closed. Before the music begins, the facilitator will read aloud the opening concepts.

1. Look inward beneath the skin and the muscles. Focus on the bones: large, small, long, short, straight, and curved. Now see and feel all of the body's joints: elbows, knees, hips, ankles, wrists, fingers, toes, and jaw.

2. Imagine invisible strings on all the joints. The strings lead outward like those on a marionette. The strings will be triggered by the music accompanying the warm-up.
3. When the music begins, be aware of the joints; emphasize them while moving through the room. Let the music "tug" at the strings and slowly move the joints. Some tugs might be small, some more intense. Allow the strings to pull the joints and increase (deepen) the angularity of the body's shape.
4. Work all the joints (angles) in the body. Feel suspended (held) in space by the strings, then release the shape and move through the room until the strings pull taut and pull the body into another suspended angular shape.
5. Energize (mentally and physically) the pointed, angular beings and abstract positions.
6. When the music finishes, stay silent and stand in neutral position for several breaths.

Internal Exploration of Curves

MUSIC SELECTION
Track 20

1. Look inward. Become aware of all the soft curved and circular areas of the body: round bones, muscles, and organs. See them and touch them with internal awareness: skull, rib cage, pelvis, eyes, nasal cavities, tongue, throat, ears, lungs, heart, kidneys, and other vital organs. Look even deeper and see and feel millions of cells moving and pulsing in circular microscopic clusters.
2. Imagine curling, rounding, and smoothing away all points and edges; melt all of the hard, sharp bone until there is nothing but soft living muscle and tissue. A pebble tossed into a pond will cause ripples to spread across the pond's surface. The curving motion of one body part will affect the surrounding muscle and tissue.
3. Respond to each curl like ripples on the water. Feel the rounding motion penetrate internally; let it spiral downward and inward into the cells.
4. When the music begins, initiate a rounding, curving, curling, or rolling movement. Move on the spot or travel through the room, but always rounding and curving.
5. At anytime, hold a position and deepen the curves. It may affect the outward shape, but focus on working internally.
6. Let the curves be concave and convex and complex variations of the two. Use stillness to explore how deep each curve can penetrate.
7. When the music ends, slowly uncurl. Lie on the floor or stand in neutral position for several breaths.

External Exploration

In two groups, repeat the internal explorations. After both groups have watched the other work, discuss.

Group Reflection

Internally as a performer and externally as a viewer, everyone should contribute an observation about how this exploration differs from the exploration in exercise 1.1.

Creation and Presentation

Work in ensembles of four. Create a dance inspired by the basket and movement elements from the other exercises in this chapter. Facilitators may assign this dance to be developed over 2 weeks; ensembles can schedule extra creation and rehearsal time outside of class. Or the dance can be short and fulfilled in one class period. There's no maximum length for the choreography, but be certain the piece is memorized. It will be manipulated spatially later on, so it's important to know the choreography.

These are the required elements for the dance:

- Use angular leaps (at least two variations).
- Use a traveling pattern in which the bodies and the path they travel on curve and spiral.
- Use two different movement phrases exploring the space between dancers.
- Use two movement phrases focusing on symmetrical movements (individually, in partners, or with all ensemble members).
- Use additional movement ideas created by the ensemble.

Present the pieces, discuss, then work on the performance variations.

Group Reflection

- Was there a strong inside and outside component to the choreography?
- How many of the dances started with dancers at the corners and finished swirling in the center? How many started in the center and worked outward?
- Think back to the illustrations of mosaic patterns from exercise 1.3 and how distinctive patterns were created by highlighting certain tiles. Now explore a variety of ways to reconfigure the choreography.

Performance Variation 1

Look at the two illustrations in student journal 1.4 (also figure 1.7 in the book).

1. In the blank circles, work on your own to rearrange the geometric elements of the basket in two other ways.
2. Meet with ensemble members and compare the drawings.
3. Rework the original choreography so that it matches one of the drawings (or combine ideas from several drawings).

4. The new choreography should contain the same elements as the original dance, only now the spatial relationship is different and that relationship may dramatically affect the timing, dynamics, and order of movement sequences. Take 20 to 30 minutes to work, then present the rearranged dances and discuss the process.

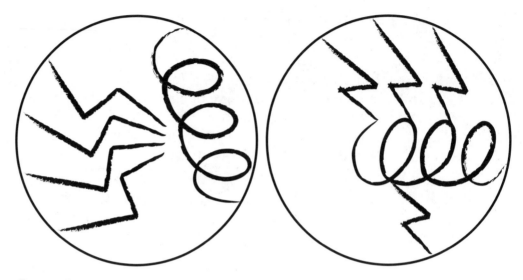

Figure 1.7 These two illustrations are examples of how the basket's angular curved element can be rearranged.

Group Reflection

The members of each ensemble should present the drawing they used for rearranging their choreography as they answer the first question followed by comments from the audience in response to the second question.

- How did you rearrange the basket's elements? How did those changes affect the original choreography?
- From an audience's point of view, did the changes highlight or diminish any of the following elements?
  - Dynamic energy of the angular lines
  - Dynamic energy of the curves and circles
  - Symmetrical elements
  - Negative and positive spatial relationships

Performance Variation 2

MUSIC SELECTION
Track 7

1. Unweave the basket dance. Divide the ensemble into two groups of two. Both pairings have the same movement information to work from, but each duet will manipulate the elements as they choose.
2. Manipulate the elements from the original quartet and rework them to create a duet.
3. Get another blank piece of paper, fold it into four equal quarters, and use the four spaces to help you plot out ideas for making the duet.

4. Take 20 to 30 minutes to rework the choreography. When everyone is ready, present it.
5. Both halves of the original ensembles should perform after each other. This will help articulate the variations used when the quartet was transformed into duets.

Group Reflection

Each pair should respond to the first question; follow that with a general conversation regarding the second question.

- List three things you did to rework the quartet into a duet.
- While dancing, did you still see or feel the other members of the original quartet? If yes, did you sense their presence at a specific time or place?

Performance Variation 3

Unweave the basket even further. Create a solo. Use only choreographic material from the original dance.

Present solos one at a time with the music, then perform the pieces again in silence.

Final Group Reflection

- Was the woven basket (figure 1.6) still present in the solos? If yes, explain how. If no, what had it been replaced by?
- When the dances were performed in silence, what filled the space where the music had been?

Student Journal 1.4

All handout materials are available on the companion Web site at www.HumanKinetics.com/DanceComposition.

Arts Connections

Read the following poem.

What You Don't See
Thirty spokes share the wheel's hub;
It is the center hole that makes it useful.
Shape clay into a vessel;
It is the space within that makes it useful.
Cut doors and windows for a room;
It is the holes that make the room useful.
Take advantage of what is there
By making use of what is not.

The poem is from Tao Te Ching and is attributed to Lao Tsu, the revered Chinese philosopher who lived in the sixth century BC (the same time Byzantine artists were creating mosaics in their churches). Did the poem sound modern and abstract? On first reading, it may have appeared somewhat abstract, but it's quite straightforward. Space is all around us: between your fingers and toes, between words in this sentence, between the walls of the room. Without the nothing of space, there would be no room for us.

For more information about Tao Te Ching and to read translations of the 80 other verses, go to www.taoteching.org.

One visual artist who was fascinated with negative and positive space was M.C. Escher (1898-1972). You're probably familiar with the works of the Dutch artist. In the past four decades his prints have appeared in calendars, postcards, pop-up books, and puzzles. I've always liked Escher's work because it makes a person look more deeply at shapes and space. Go to the Web site www.mcescher.com, click on the Picture Gallery link, and select Switzerland and Belgium 1935-1941. On that page, look for *Sky and Water I* (one of Escher's best-known woodcut prints). You could describe it by saying that out of the spaces between individual birds flying in a flock, fish appear. Or you could say that out of the spaces between individual fish swimming in a school, birds appear. Escher was a master of shape and space: Backgrounds became foregrounds shifting back and forth (or within and without), creating a symmetrical infinity.

Exercise 1.5 Traditional Brush Painting

MUSIC SELECTION
Silence and track 8

Becoming Brush, Paint, and Canvas

The exercise develops movement dynamics and demonstrates the convergence of visual art and dance. The brush is the extension of the artist and is instilled with energy that paints the air with movement.

Observation

Look at the details of brush strokes in the photographs in figure 1.8. Notice the differences in attack, liftoff, thickness, opacity, and flow. A single line or one simple brush stroke speaks volumes. It can be strong and forceful, fluid and undulating, a whisper, a shout, a stutter, a sigh.

Internal Exploration

MUSIC SELECTION
Work in silence

1. Work with a partner. One person is the artist, and the other is the paint.
2. Find a space in the room away from others.
3. Decide who will be the artist first and who will be the paint. (After several minutes, switch roles so each person experiences both aspects of the exercise.)

Figure 1.8
Japanese brush paintings.
Barry Prophet, photographer. www.pomer-prophet.com.

4. The person in the role of paint should start in neutral position gazing inward and do this work with partially closed eyes or while looking downward. The artist will make sure the paint never collides with another dancer or bumps into the wall.
5. The role of paint is to respond to the artist's brush strokes. Feel and simultaneously move to the artist's touch with movements as fluid as paint. Respond to the individual qualities of each brush stroke: heavy, light, thick, thin, wavy, sharp, and so on. There's no time to think or analyze how to respond; move like paint on canvas—instantaneously. Enjoy the sensation of outside stimulation. Give up any idea of controlling the situation. Paint doesn't think; it can only respond.
6. The role of the artist is to create the stimuli for paint's movements. Create as wide a variety of stimuli as possible. Brush paint's body (torso, arms, legs, head) using hands and fingertips. Apply a variety of weights and motions; work strokes up, down, in curves and angles, with quick dabs and long, undulating lines.
7. The dancer in the role of the paint will respond to the information received and translate it into movement.
8. The artist cannot anticipate how the paint responds to each stroke. Allow the paint to settle into stillness before painting another line. Once the dancer portraying paint has finished moving, the artist should activate the paint with another brush stroke.
9. Change roles after 3 to 4 minutes.

External Exploration

MUSIC SELECTION
Work in silence

Half of the class performs the exercise while the other half observes the working pairs. Allow 3 to 4 minutes for the first pairs of dancers to work in each of the roles, then those who had been moving may sit and observe while those who'd been watching perform.

Group Reflection

- Everyone should explain which of the two roles they preferred exploring and why.
- From an audience's and performers' experience, did certain qualities of brush stroke prove more effective than others? If yes, what were they?
- When you were in the audience, what was the most interesting aspect of the exercise? Explain.

Creation and Presentation

MUSIC SELECTION
Track 8

It takes years of study to master the classical art of Chinese, Japanese, and Korean brush painting. Like a dancer, a master calligrapher combines mental concentration and physical articulation to create a visual image (figure 1.9).

Figure 1.9
Illustrations of classical Chinese calligraphy, (a) joy, (b) open, (c) star, and (d) bravery.

Select one of the calligraphic images from figure 1.9 and use it as the foundation for a solo choreographic study. Translate its lines (the heavy strokes, diminishing points, curves, angles, and dabs) into movement. The piece need not be long, but it should include the following elements:

- A motion or movement sequence to signify the body transforming into paint.
- Form the shape of the Chinese character.
- Use that shape three times in three different ways (such as frozen, a wavering or undulating line, or traveling using isolated movements).

Take 30 minutes to work with the music or in silence. (The music has a steady percussion line and additional melodic and textural voices. The choreography can be created in silence, rehearsed several times with music, then presented with or without music as each performer sees fit.) The solos are effective performed on their own or when two or three dancers present at the same time. Divide into four groups—those whose dance is based on each of the characters. If time is an issue, have two or three dancers from the same group perform their solos together.

Performance Note

In situations like these, dancers will start at the same time but finish differently. Hold the final shape until the music has been turned off to give those still performing the audience's full focus.

Safety Note

Assign stage areas for dancers to work in to prevent collisions.

Final Group Reflection

Before discussing the dances, all those who worked with the same image should go to the performance area and freeze in the shape of their Chinese calligraphic characters. Let those viewing compare the similarities and differences. Repeat the process with dancers using each of the characters.

- Was there a wide range of interpretation for each of the symbols? Select the most contrasting interpretations for each of the symbols and ask dancers to explain their choices.
- In the illustrations, to the right of each character is a translation. How many dancers applied the meaning of the character to the choreography? Those who did apply it explain how; those who didn't apply it explain why they did not incorporate that information into their dance.

Student Journal 1.5

All handout materials are available on the companion Web site at www.HumanKinetics.com/DanceComposition.

Exercise 1.6 Modern Painting Techniques

When Paint Hits Canvas

MUSIC SELECTION
Track 9

This is a further exploration of movement dynamics employing individual and ensemble skills. This exercise requires chalkboard and chalk or a flip chart and pens.

Humans have been drawing and painting for thousands of years on rocks, papyrus leaves, bamboo, fabric, paper, skin, and bones. Unique art forms such as Maori body tattoos and Algonquin porcupin quill embroidery have been passed down from generation to generation, but art is never static. While some artists dedicate their lives to preserving traditions of the past, others are engaged in developing new techniques and technologies.

Porcupine quills decorate boxes crafted from bark and sweetgrass made by the Algonquin First Nations.
Barry Prophet, photographer. www.pomer-prophet.com.

Observation

The exercise is based on two modern painting techniques used by abstract artists working with acrylics. Acrylic paint is different from oil, ink, or watercolor paints, from the way the paint spreads onto the canvas to the length of time it takes to dry. Artists working with acrylics approach the medium with traditional tools such as brushes and painters' knives and have developed new styles and tools to take advantage of its textural qualities and vibrant colors.

Internal Exploration

MUSIC SELECTION
Track 9

1. Find a spot in which to work two or three arm lengths away from others. The first painting technique to explore is pouring.
2. Imagine the human body is a mercuric substance capable of being poured. At the sound of the music, allow that transformation. No longer muscle and bone, let the body pour itself out onto an imaginary canvas on the floor. Extend outward until it's impossible to extend outward in any direction any farther. Rise up slowly and repeat, using different speeds and directions and from different angles. Keep working until the music finishes.

MUSIC SELECTION
Track 9

3. The next painting technique to explore is splattering. This is when the artist flicks the brush at the canvas. The result may be a splattered line or individual splotches.
4. To splatter, you must become liquid in flight, then collide and splat against an imaginary, vertically suspended canvas, a sensation similar to running and hitting an invisible wall. Each splat will be different depending on the distance between artist and the canvas, the force of the brush flick, the amount of paint, and the thickness of paint. When the body as paint hits the canvas, hold the shape for several heartbeats. Let the shape be suspended in air while the dynamic vibrations of the splat fade away. You may even feel yourself drip or melt downward before you release the shape, regroup, and try it again. Keep exploring until the music is finished.

External Exploration

MUSIC SELECTION
Track 9

This is a simple contact improvisation technique that re-creates a large, extended pouring of paint. For those who've never done contact improvisation, body surfing is a good exercise to start with.

1. Get into groups of five.
2. Four dancers lie beside each other on the floor close enough so their shoulders are lightly touching. Their heads are pointing downstage, their feet upstage.
3. The fifth person crouches stage right of the group facing stage left and then slides out lengthwise across the midsection of the four bodies. As the person slides toward stage left, the bottom group smoothly rolls in the same direction (toward stage left), carrying the body along.
4. The surfing body passes over the bottom four with her arms stretched forward. When her hands are able to reach past the bodies beneath her, she uses her hands to help her to the floor, where she immediately becomes one of the rolling bodies.
5. While the top person moves to the bottom, the farthest stage-right dancer of the four original rollers rises, turns to stage left, and slides out across the four horizontal bodies to become the new surfing body.
6. Continue the process with dancers rising, sliding, rolling, and descending.

Group Reflection

1. Compare experiences with the two internal explorations. Survey the class to see which of the approaches was the preferred one and why.
2. Before working on the choreographic assignment, complete the square exercise illustrated in student journal 1.6 (also figure 1.10 in the book) to create the two samples. Use the blank squares in student journal 1.6 to create two canvases using the same method: In the first empty square, randomly place 16 to 20 dots; in the second square, connect groupings of the dots into poured and splattered shapes.

Creation and Presentation

1. Get into ensembles of 8 to 10 to create a large choreographic canvas.
2. Use body surfing to communicate a large, sustained pouring and individual dancers to communicate splatters and smaller pours.
3. Make sure the piece contains the following elements:
   - Body surfing. Try applying different speeds and textures (see what happens when the top dancer bubbles, splashes, slithers, or oozes as he or she is rolled along).
   - Individuals splatter and pour in different directions, tempos, and weights.
   - Find two other ways of traveling to represent paint independently, in pairs, or as a mass.

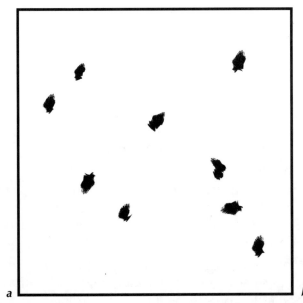
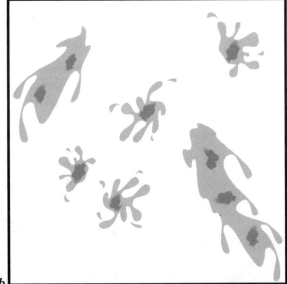

Figure 1.10 Connecting the dots. The illustrations represent (a) a canvas with randomly scattered dots and (b) a canvas where those same dots have been replaced with pours and splatters.

4. Use one of the drawings created by an ensemble member as inspiration or foundation for the final position, which will be recorded by one of the viewers and referred to in the final group reflection.

Final Group Reflection

- Look at the drawings of the finishing positions of all of the pieces. In what ways did the ensembles paint their canvases differently? Discuss the strengths and weaknesses.
- What new ways of moving as paint did the ensembles explore? Identify the most successful ones and discuss ways of evolving it further.

Arts Connection

You can visit great modern art in online galleries at the following sites:

- Museum of Modern Art in New York: www.moma.org
- Museum of Contemporary Art in Los Angeles: www.moca.org
- Tate Gallery in London, England: www.tate.org.uk/modern

Student Journal 1.6

All handout materials are available on the companion Web site at www.HumanKinetics.com/DanceComposition.

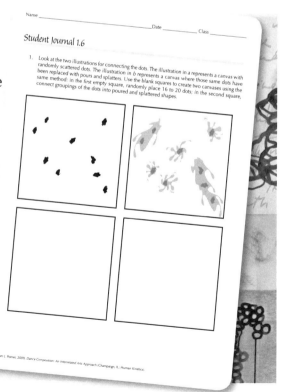

Artist Highlight Interview

Ana-Francisca de la Mora is an architect, designer, curator, dancer, and choreographer. She is a cofounder and producer of the Second Floor Collective, an ensemble of dancers, visual artists, and musicians who create multidisciplinary site-specific works. The other members of the collective are Alorani Martin, Natasha Myers, and Inge Tamm (choreographers and dancers); Robert Ock (musician and composer); Antonio Gómez-Palacio (visual artist); and Geoffrey Siskind (film artist).

JP: **You're an architect, designer, and dancer and choreographer. Is there a relationship between a body and a building?**

AF: There's a theory that the skin that covers the body is our first skin; a building, or our home, is our second skin; and the space those buildings are in is another layer of skin. Friedensreich Hundertwasser, a prominent artist in Vienna, Austria, also uses this image. So we inhabit the body, the buildings, the space, the streets, the city, the world. It's all different layers of spaces or skins. All of our senses are constantly informed and nurtured by the space we inhabit.

You know we don't just look at buildings; we experience them with all of our senses. When we go into a building, we feel it and listen to it; we contribute something to it. Space is holding the building and the space is created by continuously going there and impregnating, invigorating the building with different experiences. A building is maintained by the people who inhabit it, so the building continues to exist, growing and changing depending on who or what it houses: a restaurant, a yoga studio, an office. Places are not made by the objects or by an architect but out of what people create through habitation. A place is constantly in the process of construction and becoming. But if the building becomes abandoned, people stop going to it; they stop looking at it. It disappears and shuts down from our radar. It becomes an empty shell.

JP: **You're describing a very human condition.**

AF: When I was studying architecture, I still had a keen interest in dance. My architectural work, especially the theory work I was developing for my thesis, was very much informed by dance. My supervisor was attuned to my physical perspective, and he encouraged me to read a wide range of books about dance and design.

I was supposed to do a building at the end of my thesis, but they gave me special permission to do theoretical work. I explored Gothic, baroque, and modern architecture and how each of the styles moves us in different ways. For instance, Gothic buildings have larger-than-life proportions. The arches move upward; they stretch away from the earth and pull you into the sky. The Gothic arch, unlike the Roman arch, takes you away from the mundane experience to the spiritual, the infinite, the unknown. When you compare the Gothic arch to the Roman arch, you see how the Gothic arch makes the building tower skyward. My father, also an architect and a historian, was passionate about Gothic design and instilled in me, without knowing, a love for movement and dance through architecture.

JP: **When I think of Gothic architecture, I see high-vaulted ceilings.**

AF: Yes, it's all trying to suck you up off the ground. But when you look at baroque architecture, it's more based on human proportions. The marvel of Gothic is that they figured out a way of breaking the arch in two and making it into a peak that allowed them to reach high above and beyond earth-defying gravity.

I also studied the work of Italian architect Borromini. His work is extremely sensual. In his buildings, as well as those of other baroque architects, the walls seem to reach into the room and touch the space almost erotically. Baroque buildings extend the person through organic movement rather than height. Then you have modern architects like Frank Lloyd Wright. He used clean lines, lots of layers, clean planes, and light. Simply put, in relationship to dance, those are three interpretations, three choreographers exploring movement through space—three different movement languages.

JP: **Where did you study architecture?**

AF: In Mexico, where I grew up.

JP: **How did you come to Canada?**

AF: After I obtained my architect's license I read about the master's degree program at York University. I'd been so hungry, so thirsty to dance again, I knew it was something I had to do. Originally I'd thought to do a master's degree in philosophy and explore the relationship between architecture and dance theory, but when I saw the master's dance degree at York University had a multidisciplinary approach, I thought, *Yes, this is it!*

That program gave me the space to explore the common link between my two fields. Architecture is fascinating, and I'm compelled to look at space and shape and explore how solids affect space, how they move space, and how solids move those who inhabit the spaces they create. The solid material of walls and columns, like a pose by a dancer, are not the aim but the action that happens in between. Dance in alternative spaces was a natural evolution for me.

When I was dancing in Mexico City, I had the opportunity to work as a set designer and a performer for an outdoor piece. It was performed just beside the main cathedral in Mexico City on the major Aztec temple. The choreographer, Graciela Henríquez, wanted to highlight certain elements in the space, so we worked with lighting, fabric, and platforms. It made so much sense to dance outdoors and take the different parts of a building and the natural environment and let it inform the piece. I was inspired to continue to explore those connections.

JP: **And now you're choreographing site-specific work with Second Floor Collective in Toronto.**

AF: Yes, and we perform in Mexico as well.

JP: **Who and what is Second Floor Collective?**

AF: We're all creative artists who also have interests and degrees in other areas. Our focus is to work in alternative venues: to explore multidisciplinary and interdisciplinary performance possibilities. Early on we performed at the Gala for the International Dance Festival in Toronto (formerly fFida), which was in a warehouse space with concrete floors, then Dusk Dances in the park, and we just kept finding alternative spaces and presenters where we could show our work. We've been very lucky; we had 4,000 square feet of space to work with on the second floor of *The Globe and Mail* newspaper building. That's how we became the Second Floor Collective.

JP: **Tell me about the performance work you did in Mexico.**

AF: Initially we performed in a theater at the National Arts Centre. They have an experimental theater space there, a black-box theater. We worked on the choreography in Toronto, then when we got to Mexico we collaborated with visual artist Jocelyn del Río and another Mexican dance company, Serafín Aponte Danza.

JP: **How did you interact with the visual artist?**

AF: During the performance she drew on an overhead projector while we were dancing.

JP: **I love your overhead projector work. I saw you perform with projected text several years ago, and in that same concert Alorani and Inge performed with caged light bulbs swinging overhead. Both were very potent pieces of choreography.**

AF: In Mexico we used overhead projectors twice. In one piece Jocelyn was drawing, and for the other she used all sorts of tricks with different materials to create textural images and environments. When she sprayed water on the overhead projector, it appeared as if there was water everywhere: on the stage floor, on the back wall, and on the dancers. When you're dancing with an overhead projector, you disappear and become a shadow. If you approach the screen, you become a person again, but as soon as you step out three feet or more, you're a shadow again. We used many textures and materials, including almonds.

JP: **Almonds?**

AF: Jocelyn threw almonds onto the projector and one of the dancers appeared to pick them up and eat them.

JP: **So you're literally interacting with the projections, a true duet for visual art and dance! It's a great way of going from human to monumental to microcosmic size. It opens up fantastic spatial potential.**

AF: It's like doing a drawing plan for a building. The drawing is flat, but when you read it you're reading it three-dimensionally. You're constantly generating the third space, and it's the same thing working with projections and dance. The projections are two-dimensional, but by moving in them we're creating a new space, a new dimension, and a new context to the theater. That context informs our dance.

JP: **How?**

AF: That's the way our collective works. Alorani and Inge and Natasha all come from different disciplines and we are all interested in informing our dance and choreography with what we live with every day. In my case it's architecture. Inge's a biologist and so is Natasha, and Alorani is more focused on anthropology and education. As well there's Antonio, who's a visual artist, Geoff's a filmmaker, and Bob's a musician. We're all interested in the multidisciplinary application of dance.

JP: **Getting back to the notion of context, doesn't all dance require, or at least benefit from, a sense of place, a sense of topos?**

AF: Yes. And in regard to outdoor work, well, some people think you can just extract the choreography from the theater and put it outside, but it's not that simple. It's incredible how a place or site can make you feel so very small. Dancers and choreographers have to understand that the space is another dancer. You need to make it part of your dance, or you look out of place. If you take a piece you choreographed for a traditional proscenium arch theater and put it outside, it's lost because it's frameless.

JP: **The clouds dance better. You have to find a way of welcoming them in.**

AF: Exactly. You have to have spontaneity. There's a sense of risk all the time. You can't control what happens. When we work outside, it's wind, dogs, and rain. Inside the theater, we keep the improvisational energy by being very open to how the visual artist responds to the dance and, as individuals, how each dancer responds to the images.

Ana-Francisca de la Mora in "Diálogo." Visual art by Antonio Gómez-Palacio.
David Hou, photographer. www.davidhou.com.

JP: **How much do you see when the projected image is on you?**

AF: We see it quite clearly. Sometimes we dominate it; sometimes it dominates us. It's a dialogue. We always have improvisational elements in our choreography. We have to because nothing is for certain. But it's structured; we establish objectives. Sometimes we'll spend an entire rehearsal talking about motivation, asking ourselves questions about the reasons behind the movement. But it's not wasted time. It gives us a foundation to work from. We know where we're going, what we have to do. And during performance, as the images keep shifting around us, we keep our eyes open and respond to those changes within the context of established objectives and motivation.

Sometimes as a collective we just randomly choose an object or an area in the room and improvise around it for hours. It could be anything: a floorboard, a piece of string, simple things. We'll play with it endlessly, exploring every detail. And through this exploration we discover its limitations. Those limitations frame our work, and that frame gives us context, which ultimately allows us the freedom to create, interact, and improvise with each other.

Second Floor Collective's Web site is www.geocities.com/secondfloorcollective.

CHAPTER 2

New Spaces

Dance wasn't born in a proscenium arch theater. Traditionally, dancers danced wherever they were: in outdoor amphitheaters, in forest glens, around standing stones, and along rivers and streams. They danced around bonfires, under shooting stars, at daybreak, and through lunar eclipses. Temples, churches, shrines, public squares, streets, and homes were the dance settings for people of earlier times. Many contemporary dance artists are reviving these ancient traditions as a means of reconnecting dance with people's daily lives.

Arts Connection

A source of inspiration for working in alternative spaces is earthworks artist Andy Goldsworthy. He creates time-based art in natural settings (forests, rivers, fields) using natural elements such as branches, stones, and ice. Mr. Goldsworthy has created many books containing photographs of his art as it evolves and, over time, dissolves back into the environment. See Andy Goldsworthy in action in the biographical film by Thomas Riedelsheimer titled *Rivers and Tides*. For more information about Andy Goldsworthy, go to www.sculpture.org.uk/biography/AndyGoldsworthy/ to view his projects and explore other links.

Other artists, most notably Christo, create grand-scale outdoor art installations to make people notice their surroundings from new perspectives. People might pass by a building every day and never look at it, but when that same building is enveloped in hundreds of meters of fabric, people stop and stare. Suddenly the building is fascinating; people come from miles around to gaze at a building ignored for years. Now everyone notices the elegant, noble carriage of the high central dome and how the lower sections of the roof fall symmetrically on either side, like graceful, sloping shoulders. The building is transformed and the space around it is transformed. We look at space and shape with a new sensibility and see the park, the coffee shop, the sidewalk, street signs, and the sky in a new light through artist's eyes. The artist Christo, his wife, Jeanne-Claude, and their staff have wrapped, surrounded, and transformed public buildings and spaces, including the Reichstag in Berlin, Germany; Le Pont Neuf in Paris, France; and islands in the Biscayne Bay off Miami, Florida. You can read about their many projects at http://christojeanneclaude.net.

Just as visual artists are turning to outdoor time-based art, many choreographers are making dances for nontheater venues. They create dances designed to be performed in fountains, suspended from tall buildings, encased in kinetic sculptures, and performed on commuter train platforms during rush hour. As Ana-Francisca de la Mora states in her interview (pages 34-38), "All of our senses are constantly informed and nurtured by the space we inhabit." The exercises in this chapter take you out of the studio or theater and into public spaces to create dances.

Exercise 2.1 Landmarks

Creating Site-Specific Dances

MUSIC SELECTION
Sonic needs will vary

The Second Floor Collective perform "Monster."
Antonio Gómez-Palacio, photographer.

Observation
Identify the landmarks you pass by when traveling between home and the studio. The landmarks can be anything: a monument, a bicycle rack, or a large tree. On your own, list the landmarks you think would make suitable sites for dance performances.

Internal Exploration (Outside of Class)
Select three landmarks from your list. Go to each one and observe the following:

- The space around it
- The ways in which people pass through it or pass by it
- The ways in which the landmark interacts with other landmarks and interesting features in the area

External Exploration

Use three blank pieces of 8.5-by-11-inch paper, and draw rough maps of each landmark and the surrounding area and movement ideas related to each area. Here is an example:

- Draw the landmark (such as a fountain) and surrounding area (sloping hill, concrete paths).
- Write three movement qualities to use while dancing through or with the space (bubbling and splashing with water, rolling down a slope).
- Plot possible movement pathways dancers could use when they interact with the landmark (coming down the slope, traveling along the rim of the fountain, interacting with the water).

Group Reflection

As a class, compare the landmarks selected as possible alternative dance sites. Note whether the range of suggestions include the following ideas:

- Outdoor: gardens, fountain, park bench, bus shelter, sculpture
- Indoor: stairway, coffee cart, rotunda, notice board, swimming pool

Discuss the pros and cons of each of the sites.

Creation and Presentation (Creation Work Outside of Class)

MUSIC SELECTIONS
A portable CD player for music, dancer-generated sounds, or work with the ambient sounds

Get into groups of five or six. Select two contrasting landmark dance ideas to develop. Each group's selections should include landmarks with the following features:

- One indoor and one outdoor site
- Access (viewing and performing) from all sides or multiple levels for one of those sites

Before working, show the facilitator the sites to confirm that the areas are available for use. Some sites may be inappropriate because they require special permission from civic authorities. If there is a fountain on school property, permission should be relatively simple; a fountain in front of city hall might prove more challenging. Knowing the areas beforehand will help the facilitator plot a presentation schedule and ensure that students have permission to work on the sites.

Work at both of the landmarks. Explore their movement potential in the following ways:

- Interact with the landmark directly: Find ways to travel under, over, through, and around it.
- Translate its shape into movement to create a reflecting or repeating motif.
- Extrapolate movement ideas based on the site's uses.

With this new vocabulary, create a movement sequence or structured improvisation based on those experiences for each site. Each ensemble should keep a record of their work with the following information:

- Name of the landmark
- A rough sketch of the landmark, noting access points and ground quality
- List of the movement ideas explored
- Brief description of the movement sequences or structured improvisations the group has created and the reasons why

Unless the facilitator states otherwise, the dances need not be long or tightly choreographed, and each site may employ a different strategy. For example, the outdoor dance may be a 2-minute tightly choreographed sequence, while the indoor piece is a 4-minute improvised structure. What's most important is finding ways to interact with the individual spaces to convey their unique character, as opposed to arbitrarily placing a dance into a space without specific reason or intent.

The facilitator will have created a performance schedule to minimize travel time between sites. Come to these classes prepared to perform and to watch the other groups work. That means bringing the appropriate indoor and outdoor clothing until every ensemble has presented the on-site choreography.

Safety Note

Wear proper footwear and, if necessary, knee pads, gloves, helmets, and so on. As well, be sensitive to the needs of others. When working in public spaces, remember that the public has a right to be there and to be treated in a courteous manner. It may be wise to write a blurb about the project, print it, and make it available to anyone asking questions about why people are splashing around in the fountain.

Final Group Reflection

- Have a representative from each group explain why they chose their landmarks and how they endeavored to interact with them.
- Did all of the movement work significantly reflect the site? (If a group selected a landmark for its accessibility, was the element of accessibility apparent in the dance?)
- Did any of the ensembles use the same site? If they did, discuss the similarities and differences.
- How can this experience be applied to choreographing for traditional stage settings? (Possible answers are use of sets, comfort with alternative theater formats such as black box, in the round, and so on.)

Student Journal 2.1

All handout materials are available on the companion Web site at www.HumanKinetics.com/DanceComposition.

When we take dance out of the traditional theatrical space, we reach a whole new audience. It's true that some techniques lend themselves more readily than others to site work, but dance is adaptable and, like any other art form, it appears in many guises and each one has much to offer. In many cultures dance is performed in a variety of spaces: farmers' fields, aristocratic courtyards, sacred temple grounds, and old battlefields. There are dances for the seasons, dances for various times of day, and dances of reverence. So although it may appear unconventional for North American audiences to see dancers in a fountain or a public square, to other cultures it's commonplace. This isn't just true for dance; it's true for other art forms as well.

Arts Connection

In Western culture, puppets are predominantly marionettes and hand puppets, but Asian-Pacific puppetry traditions include shadow puppets (as in Indonesia, Bali, and India) and water puppets (as in Vietnam). In the latter technique the puppeteers work in thigh- to waist-deep water hidden behind a screen, which the puppets float in front of. The puppeteers manipulate the puppets using strings and rods submerged underwater while the puppets move on the water. Besides being wonderful camouflage for the strings, the water has reflective qualities that make it a magical performance environment.

Vietnamese water puppets are three-dimensional; Indonesian shadow puppets are two-dimensional. To those unfamiliar with the technique, they look a lot like cutout paper dolls. Shadow puppeteers use backlighting to illuminate their puppets' shadows onto a screen, cloth, or wall. The puppets are flat, but their shadows are lifelike. Some of them have articulated joints; their arms and legs reach out and kick, and as the puppeteer moves the puppet forward and back from the light source, the image increases and diminishes in size.

Figure 2.1a is a photo of traditional Indonesian shadow puppets; figure 2.1b is an image from the multidisciplinary production "Shuttle Dreams," which combines shadow puppets (created and performed by Mark Keetch and David Powell) and new music (composed and performed by Daria Dobrochna Kolbuszewska and Scott Wilson). "Shuttle Dreams" tells the story of a subway conductor's monotonous routine on the S-line subway in Manhattan (a subway line with only two stops) and his daydream wanderings.

Figure 2.1 (a) Cakril and Tagog shadow puppets from Java and (b) "Shuttle Dreams."

(a) David Powell, photographer. www.puppetmongers.com and (b) Barry Prophet, photographer. www.pomer-prophet.com.

Exercise 2.2 Dancing Shadows

Sculpting Space With Light and Darkness

MUSIC SELECTION
Any of the more atmospheric compositions, such as tracks 5, 15, or 16

MATERIALS: Handheld flashlights, candles, and other alternative lighting sources

Safety Note

Do not use laser pointers. Laser pointers can harm the corneas of the eyes.

Second Floor Collective perform "Inhabiting the In-Between" using light and projected images.
Adam Auer, photographer.

Observation

Lighting needs darkness in order to be effective. From darkness, lights create and define space. Think of how various types of lights penetrate darkness in different ways. With fire, the flames sway, flare, and leap randomly. Strobe lights pulse rhythmically. Headlights on cars and bicycles clear paths. Lighthouse beams signal safety. Overhead projectors enlarge images. Theatrical spotlights highlight a performer on stage.

Internal Exploration (Outside of Class)

MATERIALS: Handheld flashlight, an object (it can be human, animate, or inanimate), a darkened room

MUSIC SELECTIONS
Tracks 5, 15, or 16

Use the flashlight to study the object under various conditions of light and darkness. Place the object in a darkened room. Depending on the size of the object, it may need to be placed on a raised surfaced.

- Shine the light directly on the object. Start from a distance and then move closer and closer.
- Shine the light on one side. Light just the edge, then increase the light until half is illuminated.
- Shine the light from above as far from the object as possible, then move in.
- Shine the light from below as far from the object as possible, then come in closer.
- Move the light quickly and randomly across the room, at times across the object's surface.
- Pulse the beam on and off, illuminating different areas of the object.

External Exploration

Bring flashlights to the studio. If that room can't be darkened, the facilitator will arrange for the class to work in a room that can be darkened.

Divide into three groups. One group watches, one group works the flashlights, and one group works in the performance area where they should do the following:

- Find a spot several arms' lengths away from others.
- Create a starting shape.

Keep in mind that most of the performance area will stay dark, so visibility will be limited. Work safely—use simple shapes and actions.

The room will darken. Those with flashlights may work from any side of the performance area but should avoid being caught in the light. Those in the performance area may do the following:

- Stay frozen in the starting shape and not move.
- Slowly move from the starting position and carefully travel across the floor—avoid making fast, sudden moves while passing others.
- Stay rooted on one spot and move the upper torso quickly.
- Move in the darkness or move only when there is light.

Darken the room and do the following:

- Start the music.
- Turn on the flashlights (all together or at different times).

When working the flashlights, do the following:

- Maintain a steady beam of light.
- Pulse lights on and off.
- Move the light beam at different speeds and in different patterns or qualities.

- Focus on a specific dancer or group of dancers.
- Illuminate dancers throughout the performance area (and light areas where there are no dancers—such as the ceiling).
- Improvise with the dancers and the other light sources. Apply information gleaned from the internal observation study.

Continue moving until the music finishes. Rotate groups. Everyone should have an opportunity to explore all three aspects of the exercise.

Group Reflection

- What was the greatest challenge when moving onstage?
- What was the greatest challenge when working the lights?
- What was the most intriguing element observed in the exploration? (Did the lights act as a camera lens focusing in on specific movements or body parts for the viewer?)

Creation and Presentation

The Dancing Shadows exercise requires planning and experimentation with light sources and possible work in alternative locations.

Required Elements

- Create a duet or trio dance to be performed with alternative lighting.
- Keep the dance short (3 minutes maximum).
- You may use a stage or dance studio, or find alternative spaces: a hallway, locker room, outdoors at night (get clearance from the facilitator). Dancing in a broom closet has dramatic potential but may not provide adequate space for viewing. Choose a location that can accommodate the audience.
- Use alternative light sources such as flashlights or overhead projectors, but no laser pointers—they can damage the eyes.
- The dancers and the shadows of the dancers are the primary focus in the dance.
- Objects other than dancers may be used as well.
- Select the sound source: electronically generated, acoustically generated, spoken word, environmental sounds, and so on.
- Work out of class time to complete this project.

Each ensemble must inform the facilitator in writing of the location and light source selected for the dance and the safety precautions they plan to take. Facilitators are not responsible for providing the light source. If an ensemble wishes to use an overhead projector, they must go through the proper channels at the school. It will take more than one class to view all of the pieces, so reflect at the end of each class on that day's presentations.

Safety Note

Work safely. Don't take unnecessary risks. Always wear appropriate clothing and footwear and *be aware of all safety precautions required for the light source.*

Final Group Reflection

Ask a representative from each ensemble to explain the reasons behind their choices for lighting, sound, and location.

- Did the ensemble's choices work well in combination and individually? If one element was successful and another wasn't, discuss why this happened and how it could be amended.
- Identify the most striking moments in the pieces and discuss ways to develop them further.

Art Connection

David Parsons' solo masterpiece "Caught" uses strobe lighting and perfectly timed leaps and jumps to create the illusion of an airborne dancer. The audience never sees the dancer's feet touch the ground. It's spellbinding. For more information about David Parsons, go to www.parsonsdance.org.

Student Journal 2.2

All handout materials are available on the companion Web site at www.HumanKinetics.com/DanceComposition.

Exercise 2.3 Conceptual Dance for Alternative Spaces

MUSIC SELECTION
None

In 20th-century art, everyday objects are incorporated into three-dimensional works (such as the work of Marcel Duchamp and Claes Oldenburg) and two-dimensional works (such as Andy Warhol's Campbell's soup cans). Dancing with everyday objects isn't new. Fred Astaire and Gene Kelly created classic dance sequences working with all sorts of ordinary objects. This project takes the idea a little further.

Over 40 wrecked cars were used in "Serpentine Mounds" by Badanna Zack and Ian Lazarus at the Toronto Metropolitan Zoo.
Barry Prophet, photographer. www.pomer-prophet.com.

Observation

Design a dance for dancers, nondancers, and animated objects in a real-world setting. A great example is the 2003 film *Pretty Big Dig* by Canadian choreographer Anne Troake. *Pretty Big Dig* is a dance film without dancers; instead, it features big hydraulic steam shovels—the kind used in excavating land. All of the shovels' movements are choreographed, including traveling motions and isolated actions of the crane arm and giant scoop. View *Pretty Big Dig* and other contemporary Canadian dance film shorts at www.bravofact.com/shorts.

Internal Exploration

This is a conceptual exercise to be presented as a proposal on paper with rough diagrams or other visual enhancements. No one will be expected to implement the dance, but it should be possible if one had the time, money, and resources.

(Visual artists draw up proposals and rough sketches all the time. Renaissance genius Leonardo da Vinci compiled notebooks filled with designs that never got off the page.)

The conceptual dance proposal should include the following information:

- Where the dance will take place and why that location was selected (for example, in NASA's antigravity training room because . . .)
- Who or what will be moving and why they were chosen (astronauts, dancers, feathers, balloons)
- The vision behind the dance and what it communicates (freedom from gravity, freedom from the weight of worldly things)
- A few specific ideas for movement sequences

The written proposal should be no longer than two pages. The visual support (e.g., photos, maps, graphs, and so on) may be on a paper or typed on a computer. Work on this project outside of class. The facilitator will set a due date.

External Exploration

The proposals may be presented in one class period or over the course of several classes, depending on the schedule the facilitator has established.

Group Reflection

Survey the class to discover which three proposals the majority found the most intriguing, and discuss why.

Creation and Presentation

Divide into three groups (each group will be led by one of the creators of the three most intriguing proposals) and brainstorm strategies for actualizing the proposals. There won't be time to figure everything out, but try to sort out some of the basics:

- How to get permission to use the NASA antigravity training room
- What strategies to use to convince them to let you do the project (it's a great tourist attraction)
- Who might fund the proposal

Each group will present their proposals and then discuss.

Final Group Reflection

- Did all of the groups get the same amount of planning done, or did one group have greater challenges than the others? If there were challenges, identify the challenges and brainstorm solutions as a class.
- Why should dancers do large-scale projects like these? Why shouldn't they?

Student Journal 2.3

All handout materials are available on the companion Web site at www.HumanKinetics.com/DanceComposition.

Name _____ Date _____ Class _____

Student Journal 2.3

1. What was the most appealing aspect of the assignment?

   _____
   _____
   _____
   _____
   _____
   _____
   _____

2. How did you benefit from working on these conceptual dance projects?

   _____
   _____
   _____
   _____
   _____
   _____
   _____
   _____

3. How did the class benefit from working on these conceptual dance projects?

   _____
   _____
   _____
   _____
   _____
   _____
   _____
   _____

From J. Porter, 2009, *Dance Composition: An Interrelated Arts Approach* (Champaign, IL: Human Kinetics).

Culminating Exercise for Dance and the Visual Arts

The word *perspective* comes from medieval Latin, meaning to look closely at or look through. At the root of *perspective* is the Latin word *specere*, from which evolved numerous words related to viewing, such as *spectator* and *spectacle*. Think back on the journey described in the preface of this book—that of traveling up a spiraling path on the face of a mountain. It's obvious how fluid or subjective perspective can be. The actual land around the mountain never changes, but the traveler's view of the landscape fluctuates with every step.

When we think of the word *perspective* and its relationship to art, we most commonly apply it to visual art, specifically drawing and painting and the artist's ability to "correctly" render distance, shape, size, and depth. But depending on who is doing the viewing, "correct" or "incorrect" varies. When we look at art through the centuries, we see hundreds of examples of magnificent pieces in which the artists demonstrate significant technical ability but don't adhere to realistic or "correct" proportions and dimensions. There are numerous reasons for this, such as spiritual (religious), aesthetic, and cultural preferences. When we look at present-day art, we see the same thing: countless examples of extraordinary work in a range of media, some of which adhere to "correct" perspective and others that do not.

These two dolls show different perspectives in use of symbolism and depiction of reality. There is much to appreciate in both perspectives, the refined perfection of the Japanese Hakata dolls and the temporal, symbolic beauty of the Native American dolls. *(a)* The Japanese Hakata doll is prized for its fine detail and lifelike accuracy. These dolls are treasured family heirlooms. *(b)* Traditional Native American dolls are crafted out of organic materials and over time decay. The doll's impermanence symbolizes the child's passage from childhood to adulthood.

a b

Barry Prophet, photographer.
www.pomer-prophet.com.

What do we really mean by correct perspective? Being a relatively short person (5 feet tall, or 152 cm), I see elements of the world differently from those who are tall. I look up a lot. I see a lot of chins. Children like to stand close to me because I'm not physically intimidating. When I talk to tall people, I need to stand back a bit so I don't strain my neck. I have to adjust my stride when I walk with tall people. I know someone whose feet are so large that he wears shoes longer than my femur bone. The first time I saw his shoes, I thought, *This is impossible! How can anyone's feet be so large?* In my mind his shoes reached almost mythic proportions, like Goliath's sandals or Paul Bunyan's boots. I imagined little animals from Beatrix Potter stories living in them or Stuart Little commandeering a shoe and sailing off in it for a fine adventure. Anyone reading this who is short knows exactly what I'm talking about. Tall readers might think I'm out of my mind, but that's just their perspective.

Understanding or sympathizing with my perspective of a very large shoe isn't important. The shoe isn't my friend's art and I'm not in the audience looking at it. But what if that were the case? What would happen then? Would I be seeing something the artist intended for me to see? Would I be missing his message because I was predisposed to seeing something other than what was there because of my short person's perspective? Does it matter that my response to the shoe is profoundly different from that of the tall person beside me? Since much of art appreciation is subjective, does it really matter what I see in the shoe, as long as I enjoy or appreciate the experience? After all, doesn't everyone have a unique personal perspective that influences how he or she looks at and interprets things?

The View From Here

A Solo Inspired by a Work of Art

MUSIC SELECTION
Each dancer's choice

It's not uncommon for art gallery curators to plan group shows revolving around a specific theme. In some cases the curator assembles already-known works; in other cases the curator will invite artists to create pieces specifically for the exhibition. In the latter case, the curator gives the artists a theme or title to interpret and sometimes adds material or dimensional requirements (all pieces will be no larger than . . .). It's fascinating to see shows of this nature where dozens of artists interpret the same theme using the same materials and dimensions and come up with startlingly diverse interpretations. Such theme-based group shows are the inspiration for the culminating exercise in the Dance and the Visual Arts section. Each student will create solos inspired by a work of art.

Observation

The exercises in this section explore shape, line, space, and light. Become an image and see what the view is like from there. Begin by going back to chapter 1 and reviewing all of the photographs of art (available in color on the companion

Web site). Those works depict angles and curves, border patterns, symmetrical shapes, and so on. Any one of those images (except for the calligraphy and African basket because they've already been used in an extended choreographic study) may be used as a foundation for the solo. The selected image will provide the who, where, what, and why for the solo.

Study each image and select one to use as a foundation for a solo. Review the following ideas to help you select the image and to solidify ideas about this exercise.

- Will the view to be danced *be* the image?
- Will the view to be danced be *within* the image?
- Will the view to be danced be someone or something *observing* or *holding* or *manipulating* the image or object? (There's a world of difference between being the shoe and wearing the shoe.)
- Will the view to be danced be an abstract line or shape? (An abstract line can be a powerful image to work from—everything has a point of view.)
- Will the view to be danced be an inanimate object? (Is it an individual bead tucked in among others?)
- Will the view to be danced be an animate object? (It could be a flower.)

Exploration

How does it feel to be in the place where the view is experienced? Make sure you explore these qualities before you begin to choreograph:

- Texture (rough, smooth, sticky)
- Space (confined, suspended, ever changing)
- Emotion (awkward, embarrassed, bold; how does it feel to be a red splash thrown into the sea of calm blues?)

Creation and Presentation

Once the image is selected, do the following:

1. Create a 3- to 5-minute solo.
2. Choose the accompaniment from any musical discipline.
3. Use costumes or props.
4. Use an alternative space or lighting.
5. Create a title for the piece.
6. Write a 200-word artistic statement about the evolution of the piece: the artwork being interpreted, reasons for selecting it, and the music and costume or props (if using them), and any other pertinent references to give the viewer a sense of "the view from here."

    Keep a diary while working; the notes will be a source for the written assignment.

7. This solo may be evaluated with the use of the rubric or self-evaluation forms found on the Web site. As the culminating exercise for part I you are expected to incorporate ideas explored in the preceding exercises. The solo should demonstrate use of many of these elements:

    - Angles and curves
    - Shape and space
    - Symmetry and asymmetry
    - Attack and energy (remember the modern painting techniques of pour and splatter)
    - Lighting ideas

The facilitator needs to know everyone's image selection. If the choreography is for an alternative space, individuals must obtain permission to use the space and then inform the facilitator. This will help in the performance scheduling. (If many students are working with the same image, it may be interesting to present them on the same day to compare the interpretations, or the facilitator may wish to space them out over several days.) Each performance session should feature five or six pieces followed by a group discussion of the work. Make sure the artistic statements are ready for distribution before the performance.

Final Group Reflection

Audience members will have had time to read the artists' statements before viewing the dances.

- Discuss whether the statements add to the appreciation of the performance.
- Were any of the interpretations surprising? If yes, why?
- Do you think the performer clearly communicated the intended interpretation of the theme? If not, suggest ways to communicate the interpretation more clearly.

Self-Evaluation for Dance and the Visual Arts

All handout materials are available on the companion Web site at www.HumanKinetics.com/DanceComposition.

Rubric for Culminating Exercise for Dance and the Visual Arts

All handout materials are available on the companion Web site at www.HumanKinetics.com/DanceComposition.

Artist Highlight Interview

Lin Snelling is a prolific artist: dancer, choreographer, vocalist, writer, and sought-after teacher of movement, improvisation, and voice. She's performed with many dance companies, including the internationally celebrated Montreal-based dance theater company Carbone 14 (artistic director Gilles Maheu), with whom she worked and toured from 1989 to 2001 and is currently an assistant professor of Movement at the University of Alberta, Canada. Lin's body of collaborative multidisciplinary works redefines the boundaries between dance and the other arts.

Lin Snelling
Michael Reinhart. www.quebec-elan.org/showcase/display/portfolio/71.

JP: **I know when I ask you, "What's up?" you'll always have a new project to tell me about, so, what's up?**

LS: I've been working with visual artist Shelagh Keeley, and it's been amazing. The first day we went into the studio and did a movement practice together and then we both drew. Afterward we talked, danced, drew, and talked some more. By the time we finished, there were pages of notation and drawings on the wall; and the next day when we came back to the room, it was so satisfying because the drawings were still there! I could refer to them, and that's quite a wonderful thing for a dancer; normally everything disappears as soon as we've done it. I don't work with video, so my process is how I remember, either through my body or notation, or my own daily sense of remembering, and that's a very personal activity.

JP: **Every art form has limitations. When we cross over into another discipline there's often a feeling of freedom, of suddenly being able to do things one couldn't do before.**

LS: Yes, and it's interesting when different art forms get together. You have wonderful discussions and become involved in each other's process. And really, there's nothing new; we're all reinventing

JP: **Absolutely. Visual artists interpret what they see and present their interpretation through a variety of media, while actors, dancers, and musicians interpret the text, composition, and choreography and bring it to life.**

LS: What's interesting about visual artists and writers is that their practice is very private; our practice has a collective element. There's a sense of personal depth and responsibility in a visual artist's or writer's process because they question and requestion themselves alone, whereas we do that in a room with other people. At times that can defuse the work and prevent it from going deeper, but at the same time working with others stops us from feeling so isolated, so singular.

JP: **So, was it difficult to balance between your collective process and Shelagh's private process?**

LS: Shelagh is a wonderful collaborator. I've always liked her work because it deals with the body. She has a direct way of making lines that reflects a rigorous practice of trusting her intuition. This may seem like a paradox, rigor and intuition, but it's not really. It's hard to trust the messy thing, the odd or gentle line on paper, the vulnerable reality of attempting to capture something. I first met her 25 years ago. We've kept in touch all this time, then 2 years ago we happened to be in Antwerp together. She was presenting at a gallery and I was creating with Guy Cools, a dramaturge from Belgium. We met in a studio for a day and from that meeting, from that one day in the studio, we created a book. Shelagh drew and I spoke and she put it together with writing we had exchanged some years earlier about making art and our love for this act. We called the book *Drawing Space*.

The second book we created is called *Performing Book*. Basically it's an open notebook on the walls of a room. The first chapter is called "Kardia: A Space for the Heart." We perform to one person at a time. This was a proposition of Shelagh's because she said, "Reading a book is intimate—it should be performed intimately." And I said, "What about two or three people?" But Shelagh said, "No. One person is not two people. Two is different from one." I knew she was right, but the performer in me said, "But don't we want *everyone* to see it?" Shelagh was insistent and it was her conviction that led us to develop this intimate performance experience, which turned into something quite extraordinary.

JP: **How did it work?**

LS: The walls of the room became an open notebook containing spoken, written, drawn, and found images about the place of the heart in our lives, in our bodies, and in our histories. We invited each person to go into the room alone and told each person to spend as much time as he or she liked. We said, "You can write, you can draw, you can look, perhaps dance if you wish; and when you're done you can come and get us." So when they finished looking at the book privately, they opened the door and invited us back in. Then we went in and performed the book, often using the point of entry the person had made. If they had moved a chair, we'd start from there. If they had done a drawing or written something, the drawing or the text would be our departure point. That was how we reopened the book into a performance—it was different every time.

JP: **How did Shelagh participate in the performance?**

LS: We decided to bring books to the room that inspired us. Shelagh wrote down phrases from an assortment of those books and put them on the walls of the room with the drawings and with our own writings. While we performed, she would read, draw, sit and watch, or sometimes rearrange the papers on the wall. She was definitely part of the performance.

JP: **How long did the performance element of the project last?**

LS: We performed it for a week, five times a day. We did 34 performances, and one of those performances was for a class of 10 theater students. They were the exception, the only group that participated.

JP: *The Performing Book* **is a very different experience from your other collaborative pieces, but the underlying similarity is the improvisational element. You're a great improviser. Have you always been interested in improvisation, or was there something that motivated you to take that leap into the unknown?**

LS: I think it was back in the early 1980s when I was studying at Toronto Dance Theatre and one of our teachers, Gordon Dowton, encouraged improvising—how to listen, how to build, how to work collectively—and there was another fabulous teacher, Nancy Ferguson. As soon as I discovered this way of working, there was no going back. Improvising lit something up in me energetically and intuitively; it made sense to me.

JP: **Where had you been dancing before then?**

LS: Well, I graduated from Ryerson University in 1981, where I received a degree in journalism. I've always enjoyed writing and it's often my writing that inspires my dancing or vice versa!

JP: **How did you go from journalism to dance?**

LS: I fell into it, literally. I was up at York University and happened to walk into one of their big, beautiful dance studios. It was empty, and I fell in love with the empty space.

JP: **So many people are afraid of empty spaces.**

LS: It was very strange. I walked into the room on my own and I thought, *If I could spend my whole life going in and out of rooms like this, it would be amazing.*

JP: **So you hadn't planned on becoming a dancer?**

LS: No. I'd studied ballet and gymnastics, with no serious plans to pursue it, but I just kept going toward things I liked. When I discovered improvising, both vocally and physically, I discovered I could direct myself. It was about making decisions and taking responsibility for them in both a rigorous and intuitive fashion.

Improvising is a practice you learn by experience in the studio and on the stage. How the body navigates time and space is based on the dancer's intelligence and inherent understanding of constructing and deconstructing moments in time. The clarity of the choice reflects the thought process of the dancer, whether it is improvised or choreographed. This is a practice. The conscious and unconscious activity of paying attention to these choices in time reflect on a dancer's maturity and experience.

Working with Gilles Maheu and Carbone 14 gave me many things I am very grateful for, one of which is a sense of personal and collective responsibility toward working together to get closer to a vision Gilles had for each show he created. He directed with a great deal of trust in his actors and their abilities to question him in the creation process. Gilles believed very strongly in the body's ability to transport the imagination of the actor and the audience. We worked very hard and Gilles asked us to improvise, to remember, to collectively create, to search, to change, to fail, to reveal; and there was always this arrival to a point of exhaustion where there was nothing left to resist.

It can be brutal but very beautiful, and it was all in a day's work. There was a sense of exhaustion and extreme joy when all the work in the studio created these moments of grace. Brief as they were, we all recognized them and there really are no words for those moments, but they are why I keep dancing.

JP: **And teaching—you lead movement workshops for dancers, actors, and vocalists. Where do you feel the commonality between those art forms begins?**

LS: With breath. Breath is movement. When we listen to breath in the body, we're listening to movement. The body isn't still; it's active and full of energy. So starting with the breath is actually starting from the center of all movement. It's important to understand the anatomy of breathing: where the diaphragm is, how it works, how it's so beautiful and diaphanous. Then there is the beauty of making sounds, the beauty of just yawning. Yawning opens the body up. It releases the jaw, releases the hip joint, and helps the body expand and settle.

So I'll start my classes lying on the floor with lots of breathing and sounding and yawning, and we'll mix them up and allow the movement of the face to be part of the beauty of the body's movements. We shouldn't cut ourselves off at the neck or put corsets on our mouths as movers, which often happens in dance. Movement has a delicious silence, but we recognize silence by allowing ourselves to be noisy. So if we never engage in making sound, we won't get that magical silence. I like to work through both sides of the spectrum.

We play with vowels and consonants—how the body sounds and what I call translations, which is taking movement and gently translating it into an invented language and then gently translating the invented language into a text. Eventually the invented language can be gently translated into a melody, and the melody becomes an interlocking part to other interlocking parts in the room that are building at the same time. Then we're singing altogether as an orchestra, and when we're finished, the resonance of that singing translates into the body as movement vocabulary.

One thing translates into the other. They're all states that reflect the interconnectedness and intelligence of the body. One of the lovely things about working with sound is that it goes out into the room and you can hear it, just as dancing has its sense of resonance, its own kind of voice that is visceral.

I've started to use musical language as improvisational movement language. I'll ask dancers to make harmonic choices, to explore dissonant relationships, or allow themselves to be melodic or rhythmic, separately or with others. That's a direct translation you can make between musical language and movement language—between the body and sound. And really, how can you separate them? Sound and bodies resonate: We vibrate, we breathe.

My vision as a dance artist over the past 20 years has been constantly honing the musical, experiential, intuitive, technical, energetic, and anatomical intelligence the body offers by dancing. My work as a choreographer, improviser, teacher, and performer plays with and listens to the practical and paradoxical intelligence of the body. Like following a musical score, this listening integrates the body with the place. The place could be a theater, a factory, a photograph, an intersection, a landscape, a drawing, a café, or a dance studio. The body offers an intuitive frame that can spiral perspective, dynamic, and dimension into something we can all feel deeply. We are touched by the resonance of how a specific body moves into a specific place. This moment-to-moment relationship to place gives dancing a sense of impermanence that is tangible. Touching this timing in the body can bring us closer to a very ordinary sense of magic and longing. We all have a body from which to tell the time.

PART II
Dance and Music

To study the history of music is to study the history of humans. Music archives discovered in archaeological digs date back through the ages. There are wonders such as 100,000-year-old single-note whistles made from bird bones in Ireland, a 35,000-year-old multiple-note flute made from the tusk of a woolly mammoth in Germany, lithophones (stone percussion instruments) from the Neolithic period discovered in Vietnam, and intricately carved clappers and rhythm sticks from ancient Egypt. The didgeridoo dates back to at least 20,000 BC. The dronelike wind instrument is still played in the rituals and celebrations of the Australian aboriginals and is popular in healing circles around the world today.

Gitanjali Kolanad (foreground) and Parmela Attariwala.
Barry Prophet, photographer. www.pomer-prophet.com.

Dancers have an intimate relationship with music. Music is our partner. It lifts us, pushes us, and stretches us. Music is a combination of sounds and silences just as dance is a blend of actions and rests. In many dance traditions the dancer is also the musician—stamping, clapping, and wearing sound-generating apparel. Composers explore sonic spatial relationship, rhythm, timing, texture, level, shape, attack, line, and direction using a myriad of musical instruments and working in countless musical traditions. Choreographers work with those same compositional elements as they apply to the human body.

Musical instruments keep evolving—from hollowed-out bird bones to double-reed bassoons. Musicians are innovators and so too are dancers. Though our instrument (the body) hasn't changed as noticeably, the way we move has. Our physicality and artistry rise to each new sonic challenge. Whether we're preserving traditions or creating new ones, dancers and musicians push and pull one another to breathtaking heights.

The choreographic exercises in part II explore music elements in exercises that develop a deeper understanding of the following concepts:

Listening skills

Internal musicality

Rhythmic impulses and patterns

Layering, spacing, and ornamentation

Tempo and textural dynamics

Tone color, note, and pitch

Found sound

Recorded and computer-assisted music

CHAPTER 3
Rhythm and Tempo

The first drum you hear is in your mother's womb. The rhythm of her heart vibrates through you, and your own heart answers back. As an infant your inner drum supports and strengthens you. You move to your inner drum, and from it you learn to recognize and respond to the complementary rhythms and vibrations around you. Before you can walk, you dance: shifting weight from side to side, from body part to body part, smoothly, erratically, sympathetically, ecstatically. Is it possible to separate the drum from the dance?

In musical terms, most drums are members of the membranephone family. Membranephones are constructed by stretching a skin, or membrane, across a frame, or shell. The thickness and flexibility of the membrane and the size, shape, and material of the frame or shell determine the range and timbre of the drum and dictate much of what is possible in playing styles. For example, a West African djembe with a water buffalo or goat hide and large, thick wooden shell has a louder, deeper voice than a clay-shelled North African darbuke with a membrane top of dried fish skin. (Other styles of darbuke have metal shells and use thicker skins.) The fish skin and rounded clay edges allow for a lighter touch and more finger dexterity than is possible with the larger, hard-rimmed djembe; while both of those drums employ hand-drumming techniques, they are different from the techniques used in playing South Indian tabla. And "skin to skin" is not the only approach to drum technique; the African talking drum, the European snare and kettle drums, Japanese taiko drums, and North American Innuit spirit drums all employ different types of mallets and playing styles. Regardless of the playing style, when you hit the drum skin, you hear the initial attack sound and a secondary sound that is the sympathetic resonance. The heart works in a similar way: It beats and your entire body responds. The lungs expand and contract, blood rushes through the veins, and every cell in the body vibrates. We are membranephones: skin stretched over a hard shell.

One style of darbuke uses a clay shell and a fish skin head while the djembe is made with a wooden shell and thicker animal hide.
Barry Prophet, photographer. www.pomer-prophet.com.

Every culture's music contains a drum. In many cultures the drum *is* the music; in others it's the foundation on which the melody and counterpoint are layered. Even music that on the surface appears to have no consistent beat contains an internal rhythm, an invisible breath or heartbeat. A whale's heart beats slower than a hummingbird's—sometimes the connecting heart line is too soft to hear or too large to identify, but it's always there.

To develop musicality, we need to develop our awareness of sound and how it moves us. Urban society is cluttered with sonic stimulation—our minds and bodies are bombarded with an audible and inaudible cacophony of sounds that make deep listening difficult. One way to start developing the skill is by unplugging the earphones and turning off the music. Walk outside and listen to the world go by. Hear and feel your heartbeat and internal rhythms and pulses while you walk; see and feel how they connect with what's going on around you. Can you feel the rumble of the truck before and after it comes into view? Does the rumble heighten or mask other sounds and vibrations? What part of your body responds most readily to the truck? Is it a different part of you that responds to the sound of birds? How do the tempo, length, and weight of your walk respond to those sounds? How does your heartbeat respond? Are your thoughts affected? Does your focus change? How is what you're experiencing different from your response to music that's on the radio?

We're always drum dancing—the body is filled with rhythmic pulses. But do we always hear them and feel them? Do we listen to the drum inside us while we dance?

Exercise 3.1 Heartbeats and Drumbeats

MUSIC SELECTION
Track 10

Exploring Sounds and Silences

This exercise expands your musicality by developing your deep-listening skills and awareness of complementary and contrasting rhythms, textures, and tones in percussive music and the internal rhythms of the heartbeat and breath.

Percussionist David Thiaw.
Barry Prophet, photographer. www.pomer-prophet.com.

MUSIC SELECTION
Track 10

Observation

The entire body responds to audible sounds and sonic vibrations. To observe this, lie down on the floor with your eyes closed.

1. Listen to the silence and ambient sounds of the room for 2 to 3 minutes.
2. Listen to the music (track 10).
3. Listen to the silence and ambient sounds for 2 to 3 minutes.

Before continuing with the exercise, sit with the rest of the class and discuss what people heard in the silence before listening to the composition, the silence after listening to the composition, and the silences within the composition. Were the silences different or exactly the same? If they were different, discuss how and why.

Internal Exploration

Play the music four more times; each time, explore the composition through different areas of the body. Always allow 30 to 60 seconds of silence and external stillness between explorations.

1. The first time the music plays, move only the upper torso, arms, hands and fingers, neck, and head.
2. The second time the music plays, move only from the waist down: lower torso, legs, feet, and toes.
3. The third time the music plays, move only the head and neck: eyes, eyebrows, mouth, jaw, and nose.
4. The fourth time the music plays, move the entire body.

Musicians can hear their music while they're playing, but dancers can't see the dance as they move. That is one of the reasons all of the exercises contain internal and external exploratory steps.

External Exploration

1. Get into groups of four. Each dancer in the ensemble will represent one of the movement variations.
2. Ensembles will present one at a time while the rest of the class watches.
3. When ensembles are in the performance area, make sure those presenting the first (upper body) and third variation (face isolation) are positioned so that they're visible to the viewers. Dancers presenting the variations with greater mobility should avoid blocking them.
4. Once the ensemble has assumed its starting position, play the music. After all of the ensembles have presented, sit together and discuss the experience.

Group Reflection

- Was there an orchestral sense to the movement ensembles? If yes, how and why? (For example, the bodies have different ranges of mobility just as instruments in an orchestra have different sonic ranges, thus creating a sense of harmony.)
- During the presentations, was any variation (upper body, face, and so on) or any specific ensemble or individual more eye catching than others? If yes, discuss why.
- The music contains rests (silences). Were there visual rests? If so, how did they affect the dance?

During the discussion, some people might have said that there was so much movement that they found themselves watching the quietest dancer performing the face isolations downstage left. Conversely someone else might have found that the face isolation was completely lost among the larger actions. When musicians arrange a piece of music, they take into account each instrument's sonic properties: its range, pitch, and volume.

Exploration Variation

Get into larger ensembles of five to seven. The four variations will no longer be equally presented. Take 1 to 2 minutes to determine how the variations should be divided within the ensemble (for example, four dancers work the face, and the other three work the other variations) and create an opening position. Present, and after all ensembles have presented, do a survey to see whether these variations had a greater or lesser sense of the following:

- Rhythmic exploration
- Harmony (layering)
- Energy and dynamics
- Lyricism

Discuss the strengths and weaknesses of each ensemble's choice.

Creation and Presentation

Create a short (60- to 90-second) solo employing a range of rhythms and dynamics using elements of the four movement variations: full-body movement and upper-body, lower-body, and facial isolations. The choreography is to be created and performed without musical accompaniment. Stay internally connected to the rhythmic, dynamic, and textural choices. Become the music and the dance.

Present the solos individually or, if there are time constraints, two at a time (in which case the dancer finishing first freezes in her final shape until her partner is finished). After the presentation, discuss these questions:

- The pieces were performed in silence, but were there moments when you heard music?
- Did you hear the same instrument or sound for all of the movements or body parts, or did certain actions and isolations generate specific sonic resonance? In other words, did the facial isolations and the lower torso work "sound" the same? If not, how did they differ?

If class time is not a concern, it's interesting to see everyone present the solos individually, then again in groups of three and up. See if groups can be structured in various ways. For example, a group of seven dancers can present. Three are at center stage while the others are on their own in upstage or downstage corners.

Student Journal 3.1

All handout materials are available on the companion Web site at www.HumanKinetics.com/DanceComposition.

Arts Connection

The human body is mostly water, and water is an excellent conductor of sound. All the sounds you hear and those you can't hear vibrate through your body. Even if you are hard of hearing or deaf, you are a full participant in the drum dance. Evelyn Glennie, one of the United Kingdom's top performers and interpreters of contemporary percussion, is deaf. A visually dynamic performer who physically embodies the music, she performs with symphony orchestras, is an internationally respected recording artist and composer, teaches music (including deep listening skills), and is a sought-after motivational speaker. In 2007 she was awarded Order of the British Empire (OBE) and is now Dame Evelyn Glennie. *Touch the Sound*, a film by Thomas Riedlsheimer, examines this extraordinary musician's life and work. For more information, go to www.evelyn.co.uk.

Exercise 3.2 Clap Hands

Rhythmic Explorations: 5/4 and 7/4 Time

MUSIC SELECTION
Tracks 11, 12, and 13

This exercise strengthens musicality and internal rhythmic sense by exploring two time signatures not commonly used in Western music.

Most Western classical and popular music employs 3/4, 4/4, 6/8, and 8/4 time signatures. That doesn't mean Western music sounds the same. An 18th-century composition for a string quartet contains several movements, such as largo, adagio, vivace, and gigue, and each movement explores the compositional theme through a different time signature or tempo (modern jazz ensembles use a similar format). Classical composers employed this structure to create compelling works embracing a range of emotions, sonic textures, and layering, but in the grand scheme of numbers, Western music uses a relatively narrow menu of tempo and rhythms compared to other music traditions. African, South American, Middle Eastern, and Asian classical and folk music as well as European medieval music (which owes much of its richness to Middle Eastern influences) and 20th- and 21st-century experimental art music employ a wider range of rhythmic structures.

Observation

MUSIC SELECTION
Tracks 11, 12, and 13

Sit on the floor and listen to track 11. Variations for counting 5/4 and 7/4 time are spoken slowly and clearly. Count along with the patterns on this track. Repeat again, if necessary, to develop confidence.

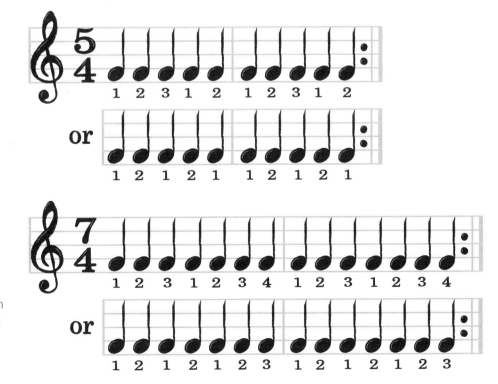

Figure 3.1 An illustration of some ways to count 5/4 time and 7/4 time.

Go to track 12. It contains the same patterns for 5/4 time but faster and without a voiceover counting. Each variation is repeated 8 times. Count along internally, and quietly tap the rhythms while the music plays. Play the track a second time if the rhythms need to be reinforced. Repeat the process with track 13, which contains faster versions of the 7/4 variations counted aloud on track 11.

If there's a need to review how to read time signatures, the top (or first) number refers to the number of beats in a bar; the bottom (or second) number shows which note value (eighth note, quarter note, or half note, for example) is equal to a single beat. The time signature of 5/4 means there are 5 beats to a bar and a quarter note gets 1 beat. Follow the patterns from tracks 11, 12, and 13 in figure 3.1.

MUSIC SELECTION
Tracks 12 and 13

Internal Exploration

Go from quietly tapping to exploring a full-body response. Work improvisationally using a variety of movement skills to respond to the rhythms on tracks 12 and 13. Integrate footwork, the torso, arms, and facial expressions.

Play each track three more times while exploring the various rhythmic pulses and dynamics through dance. Be sure to listen to the variations and respond to the change of dynamics from pattern to pattern.

External Exploration

Get into ensembles of six to eight dancers and make a circle with a diameter of at least 10 feet (3 meters). That's the space individuals will dance in. Try to position the ensembles as far away from each other as possible. Once the circles are created, do the following:

1. Pick one person to clap a rhythmic pattern in 5/4 or 7/4 time; the others join in.
2. After everyone is clapping, the person who introduced the rhythm goes into the circle to improvise a short (45- to 60-second) dance animating or interacting with that rhythm.
3. The first dancer passes the movement on by changing places with someone in the circle.
4. The clapping shouldn't stop, but it should become softer. The new dancer will introduce a new pattern in the same time signature (5/4) or different time signature (7/4), and it's everyone's job to pick up the new pattern as quickly as possible.
5. The dancer introducing the new pattern should keep clapping until the rhythm is established; then that dancer should begin to dance. After 45 to 60 seconds, the second dancer trades places with another, and the process continues until everyone has contributed a pattern and performed in the center.

Group Reflection

Discuss these questions before moving on to the next step.

- Did the polyrhythmic environment of the room feel cacophonous or harmonious?
- Was it appealing, irritating, or a mixture of both? Discuss the sonic and visual sensations experienced throughout the exercise. Many African cultures use polyrhythmic structures in their music to create rich compositions of overlapping rhythms that ebb and flow in and out of phase. Some 20th-century minimalist composers, such as Steve Reich and John Adams, were profoundly influenced by these compositional techniques. "Drumming" (Reich) and "Shaker Loops" (Adams) are contemporary classic compositions that employ phasing techniques.
- Did the skills you developed in the previous exercise help? Did you feel compelled to move on every beat, or did you interact with the rhythmic pattern by working off the beat or in between the beats by using suspended motions or moments of stillness?
- The previous exercise also highlights ways to animate various parts of the body, including facial muscles. Do a general show-of-hands survey to discover how many people remembered to use facial movements in this exercise.

Creation and Presentation

Work in small ensembles of three or four. Half of the groups will work exclusively in 5/4 patterns, and the other groups will work in 7/4. Create an ensemble dance sequence incorporating the following ingredients:

- Create at least three distinct rhythmic patterns by placing emphasis on alternative beats. (For example, for 5/4 it's **1**, 2, **1**, 2, **1** and **1**, 2, 3, **1**, 2. For 7/4, it's **1**, 2, **1**, 2, **1**, 2, 3 and **1**, 2, 3, **1**, 2, 3, 4.)
- Use clapping, stomping, finger snapping, voice (but avoid using actual words), and other ways of generating the sonic aspect of the rhythmic patterns. These patterns may be performed in place and while traveling.
- Perform a sequence of full-body movements in silence.
- Use a variety of spatial relationships between ensemble members. Travel across the floor in various formations, work close together and then move in different directions, and so on. Space is an important element in music—it's the space between beats that creates rhythm, the space between notes that creates harmony and melody, the space in the room through which sound reverberates. Remember the Lao Tsu poem about space from exercise 1.4 (on page 24).
- The piece should be repeatable.

Everyone has a wealth of ideas and should contribute equally to the creation of the work. The sequence need not be longer than 1 minute, which doesn't mean there can't be improvisational elements. For example, a structured improvisational element can be inserted after six choreographed sets of 7/4, allowing half of the ensemble members two sets to improvise while the other half travel using a choreographed clap and stomp sonic and movement pattern. After everyone has had a chance to improvise, the opening six sets are repeated. Some ensembles may prefer to choreograph the entire sequence; either way is fine as long as the dance doesn't end in a fixed "ta-dah!" pose that can't smoothly reconnect to the beginning of a movement phrase.

After 20 minutes, ensembles should be ready to present. There are three ways to view the ensemble pieces. All ensembles do the first variation. Half of the class does variation 2, and the other half of the class does variation 3.

- Each ensemble will perform the sequence two times through (without stopping in between) while the other ensembles watch.
- Two ensembles present at the same time; each ensemble represents a different time signature.
- Create new performance groups containing individuals from the original ensembles (two working in 5/4 and two in 7/4) yet no two dancers from the same original ensembles.

Final Group Reflection

- Discuss some of the outstanding sonic and choreographic elements (unique vocalizations, playful work with accent beats, body isolations, and so on) presented in the first variation.
- Discuss the successes and challenges of the second performance variation. (Did it create powerful polyrhythmic choirs or dramatic tension and intensity between rival groups? Was it difficult to avoid interfering with other people's pathways?)
- There were unique elements and challenges in the third variation. It's difficult to keep internal time without the support of the others, so how did dancers resolve this? What was it like to watch? (Were there disjointed moments that suddenly gelled together and just as suddenly broke apart? Was that exciting, chaotic, or anything else? Describe.)

Arts Connection

Latcho Drom, the 1993 film by Tony Gatlif, features some of the most extraordinary musicians and dancers of Roma, or gypsy, traditions from around the world. The film begins in Rajasthan, the birthplace of the Roma people, then follows their migration to Egypt, Turkey, Romania, Hungary, Slovakia, France, and Spain. Near the beginning of the film is a scene in Rajasthan in which women are seated in a circle playing complex rhythms on hand cymbals attached together by long cords, and in the silences the cymbals twirl overhead. It's absolutely breathtaking. It's a brilliant documentary and a valuable resource for anyone interested in cultural dance or ethnomusicology. Go to http://tonygatlif.free.fr or do a Web search for "Latcho Drom" which will also lead you to several sites where you can view excerpts of the film, read reviews, and study Romany culture.

Student Journal 3.2

All handout materials are available on the companion Web site at www.HumanKinetics.com/DanceComposition.

Name _____ Date _____ Class _____

Student Journal 3.2

1. A simple rhythmic pattern for 5/4 is 1, 2, 3, 1, 2. List two other ways of counting 5/4 time.

2. A simple rhythmic pattern for 7/4 is 1, 2, 1, 2, 1, 2, 3. List two other ways of counting 7/4 time.

3. Explain how dancing in 5/4 and 7/4 is different from dancing in 4/4 time.

4. How has this exercise helped you strengthen the following skills?
   - Listening and counting skills

   - Musicality and performance dynamics

From J. Pomer, 2009, *Dance Composition: An Interrelated Arts Approach* (Champaign, IL: Human Kinetics).

Exercise 3.3 Variations on a Theme

Music and Movement Dynamics

MUSIC SELECTION
Tracks 12, 14, 15, and 16

This exercise explores simple shapes and motions through musical variations of sustain and attack. Before physically manipulating shapes, try manipulating a simple tune to warm up and to review the following musical elements, which are found in music from around the world and are described here using the Western classical music terms:

- *Staccato* in Italian means detached. As a musical term, it's notated by a dot placed under or over the note. The note is played with a clear attack and liftoff. The light, quick liftoff means the note is held for a little less time than its actual note value, which adds to the detached quality.
- *Legato* in Italian means bound together. As a musical term, it's notated by a horizontal bracket above or below a group of notes. The notes flow smoothly together; they are connected with no attack sound to break the stream of sound between notes.
- *Trill* means shake. It is an ornamentation in which the musician quite literally shakes the note by quickly playing the notes above or below it. Trills are notated with a small, horizontal squiggle above or below the note. Trills must fit in the allotted time value and be consistent with the composition but are generally improvised by the musician.

Figure 3.2 illustrates the Western notation for these musical terms. Think back to your experiences in exercise 1.1 of exploring curves and angles. Feel the smooth, gentle curve of the legato symbol and the tight, angular zigzag of the trill. The staccato dot reaches out to no one. It is alone, separated from the notes around it. The symbols visually translate the sonic experience. We can relate to the symbols physically as well. Deep listening can even be applied to reading music: our bodies respond to the messages each symbol sends out.

Figure 3.2 The Western music notation for *(a)* staccato, *(b)* legato, and *(c)* trill.

Observation

Hum "Twinkle, Twinkle, Little Star" four distinct ways:

1. Hum quickly and lightly with clear attack and liftoff for each note (staccato).
2. Use a moderate tempo, attack, and lift, but add ornamental trills to many of the notes.
3. Connect one note to the other (legato) to create an unbroken line from note to note.
4. Stand near two or three others and hum in different pitches (harmonics).

Internal Exploration

Create and memorize four shapes containing these required elements:

- An asymmetrical shape performed at any level containing two angles
- A low, symmetrical shape
- A middle- to high-level twisted shape
- A shape with one foot off of the floor

The shapes should be simple and easy to get into and out of (on a single beat if necessary); hold the shapes for an indefinite length of time. (Backbends and handstands aren't suitable.)

Assume a neutral position facing any direction. When the music comes on, perform the shapes using tempo, attack, and ornamentations explored in "Twinkle, Twinkle, Little Star."

Exploring Staccato

MUSIC SELECTION
Track 12

1. The first piece of music is in 5/4 time. It's one of the tracks accompanying exercise 3.2, so if you've just completed the previous exercise, you should be skilled at counting in 5/4 time. Move quickly and sharply into your shape on beat 1. Try to be frozen in your shape by 3 (at the very latest) and hold in stillness for the remaining beats of 4 and 5. On the first beat of the second set of 5/4, quickly move into shape 2, hold it until the third set of 5/4 begins, and so on.
2. After you have completed shape 4, go back to shape 1. Repeat your sequence of four shapes four times, become lighter or quicker with each repetition, then stand in neutral position and await the second music selection.

Exploring Trill

MUSIC SELECTION
Track 14

1. The second piece of music is 50 seconds long. A bell rings every 10 seconds. Move into shape 1 at the sound of the first bell, and fill in the remaining seconds until the next bell sound by pulsing or swaying, or try alternative ways of trilling a part of the shape (using an arm, for example).

2. When the second bell rings, move into shape 2 and pulse or trill this shape by animating a different body isolation (both legs, for example). Continue in this fashion until you've explored all four shapes.
3. At the sound of the fifth bell, return to neutral position and await the next piece of music.

Exploring Legato

MUSIC SELECTION
Track 15

1. The third music selection is an atmospheric piece. It's approximately 2 minutes long. There will be no sonic cues to signal movements between shapes. The goal is to work so slowly that it takes 2 minutes—the entire composition—to move through the four shapes. Sustain each action and move as smoothly as possible while traveling from shape to shape.

   When the music begins, start by slowly moving into shape 1. Don't stop at shape 1; slowly melt out of it and into shape 2. Maintain this fluid, unbroken process through shapes 3 and 4.

2. Hold shape 4 and, if the music is still playing, stay frozen. (If the shape makes it difficult for you to balance, adjust the shape to make it easier to maintain the freeze.)

External Exploration

MUSIC SELECTION
Tracks 12, 14, and 15

There are three presentation variations to explore and observe. A third of the class will present their shapes while the rest of the class watches.

Variation 1

The dancers presenting this variation will perform the three original variations, starting in reverse order with the slow legato, then using trills, and finishing with staccato, using the same spatial relationship the class used throughout the internal explorations.

1. Start in neutral position facing any direction. When the music begins, move slowly and continue as smoothly and evenly as possible (avoid even the smallest sharp or jerky action) through the four shapes. Freeze in shape 4; if necessary, modify it to maintain balance until the next piece of music appears.
2. The sound of the bell will announce the trilling music. Perform that variation.
3. Hold shape 4 until the quick, light 5/4 time for the staccato variation is played. Perform that variation and hold shape 4 to finish.

Variation 2

1. Members of the second group stand in neutral position in small, tight clusters—so tightly that individuals are almost touching each other, and each person should face a different direction and have a different line of focus.

2. The clusters themselves should be a good distance apart. This will create several distinctly separate groups of huddled dancers randomly staggered across the stage. Because of the relative closeness of the work, dancers might have to adjust their shapes to avoid bumping into each other while moving. Perform these adjustments as subtly as possible.

3. Follow the same starting and stopping procedures as the previous group. Begin with the slow (legato) movement, then the trilling variation, and finally the fast and sharp 5/4. Work carefully in the clustered positions.

Variation 3

1. The final spatial variation uses a combination of blocking from the first and second presentations. Half of the members of the final ensemble should place themselves in a tight cluster while the others work randomly scattered across the performance area. Some may face the same direction (choose whether that should be the cluster or the individual "satellites").

2. Follow the same structure as the previous groups and present the four shapes using legato, trill, and staccato qualities.

After the final group has presented, sit together and discuss.

Group Reflection

- How important was the spacing? Musically speaking, is blocking similar to the spatial relationship between notes?
- What musical dynamics did you observe in your own work and in the work of others? (For example, did the legato movement have lyricism, did the trills have playfulness, and so on?)

Creation and Presentation

MUSICAL SELECTION
Track 16

Get into ensembles of five to seven people, each ensemble consisting of a mix of members from the previous ensembles. Use the information gleaned from observing legato, staccato, and trills in the various spatial relationships from the group explorations to create a choreographic structure incorporating the following elements:

- Spatial relationships. Have varying distances between ensemble members and work with dancers facing different directions.
- Tempo and attack. Ensemble members move through their shape sequence three or four times using various mixtures of tempo and attack. For example, try legato to move into shape 1, staccato for shapes 2 and 3, legato into shape 4, then hold that shape and trill.
- Action and rest. Ensemble members may freeze in any shape at the beginning, during, or at the end of performing their shape sequence.

The musical composition is 2:58 long. Play it no more than two times while ensembles plan their choreographic structures. Afterward, each ensemble will present their work.

At the end of each piece, dancers should hold their final positions for several heartbeats to allow the silence and stillness to radiate, then release their shapes and leave the performance area.

After all the ensembles have presented, discuss the work.

Final Group Reflection

- Did the musical accompaniment support the movement work? If yes, how?
- Did the clusters transform the individual shapes? Musically speaking, did the tight clusters resemble chords? If yes, describe how.
- Were the individual dancers (those outside of the clusters) lost or highlighted? Describe them in music terms.

Student Journal 3.3

All handout materials are available on the companion Web site at www.HumanKinetics.com/DanceComposition.

Time Is a Sandwich

I want to tell you about my "time is a sandwich" theory. Years ago, one of my classes of 7- and 8-year-olds was working on a water dance we'd created over the course of several weeks of exploration and discovery. Finally we were ready to put all of our movement phrases together. I called out each of the words we had created movement phrases for, and the children responded beautifully. They bubbled, rippled, splashed, swished, and swirled. They dripped, drizzled, and poured, and rushed wildly about. The dance concluded when they made a giant whirlpool, froze, and then slowly melted out on the floor to form a calm and quiet lake.

After dancing, we sat together in a circle and talked about what we had done. (I encourage students of all ages and abilities to discuss and reflect on their movement work.) The first child to speak said, "I'm exhausted; we must have been dancing for hours." "No," I replied, "it was just over two minutes." The class was stunned. "How can that be?" Another said, "It felt like forever." I sat there thinking about time and density and the fullness of the moment. That was how my "time is a sandwich" theory was born. Here's what I told them:

"The space between one minute and the next is always equal on a clock: 60 seconds for each minute, but in dance the space between one minute and the next isn't always the same. In dance, the space between one minute and the next is like two pieces of bread. Each piece of bread marks the beginning or end of a minute, and we can put whatever we want in between. A sandwich can be very thin—as simple as two pieces of bread with a single slice of cheese for its filling. That type of sandwich takes very little effort or energy to eat. A few bites and it's gone. But sandwiches, like dances, aren't always thin. They can be thick and dense with layer upon layer of lettuce, tomatoes, alfalfa sprouts, sweet pickles, cheese, turkey slices, and spicy peppers with lots of mayonnaise and mustard slathered on top. That sandwich is so big you can hardly get your mouth open wide enough to bite into it. When you do get a bite into your mouth, there are so many flavors that your tongue doesn't know which flavor to taste first. You have to really concentrate as you chew and chew and chew, and then swallow one wonderful mouthful at a time. Our water dance was just like that giant sandwich: we put so much into it that the space between one minute and the next got bigger and thicker and more exciting than two minutes of dancing normally feels. That's one of the magical things we can do as dancers: Not only can we stretch our bodies, but we can also stretch time."

Think about it—we've all experienced it—but had I not had to explain density of time to children, I would never have thought of it in such a clear and simple way. It's one of the reasons I love working with children. Their curiosity is infectious. They make me examine familiar things from new perspectives. Their need to understand keeps me looking for answers. And their acceptance, when things are clearly explained, is overwhelming. For weeks afterward they'd ask me, "How many bites?" instead of "How many beats?" when we were counting out combinations.

Now, dance doesn't have to be fast and ever-changing to stretch time. Dancers are able to manipulate time with the simplest of movements by using breath, weight, and awareness. Butoh dancers, for example, often work slowly, yet their performance energy is vibrant. You've been connecting with breath from the first exercise; let it continue to be your guide while you work at varying tempos and textures.

Exercise 3.4 Playing With Time

MUSIC SELECTION
Tracks 17, 18, and 19

One Composition, Three Tempos

MATERIALS: A watch with a second hand

The challenge of this exercise is to choreograph a short solo to a composition played at one tempo, then to adapt it to a faster and a slower tempo.

Observation

When the same movements are performed with different time allowances, the dynamics of the movements change. Think about how time can change the following experiences:

- Getting to class
- Eating a meal
- Taking a shower

Internal Exploration

Working independently, select a technical movement exercise that can be performed in 16 beats. The facilitator will call out the tempo. The first 16 beats are at a moderate tempo, then 16 beats quickly, followed by 16 beats slowly. Instead of repeating the movement on one side of the body three times, it may be appropriate to alternate sides.

External Exploration

Get into two groups (one group presents while the other watches) and repeat the exercise.

Group Reflection

- What dynamic changes did you see individual dancers make as they worked? (Their energy expanded or contracted, they changed facial expressions, they changed weight of movements or quality of attack, and so on.)
- Which tempo did you find most interesting to watch? Why?

Creation and Presentation

Create a solo for a short jazz composition for piano, bass, and drums. Have fun with the rhythmic and timing relationships; play with the backbeat, the pulses, and the melodic line. Set the choreography as specifically as possible. In this exercise it's important to work with accuracy, so be decisive and set each movement. If necessary, work on the assignment out of class.

Performance Variation 1

Once everyone has choreographed the solo, present the pieces one at a time. Afterward, discuss the contrasts in choreography and identify particularly eye-catching moments.

Performance Variation 2

Listen to track 18. It's the same composition played at a slower tempo. Rework the original choreography for the new tempo. Some movements will be easy to lengthen and extend; others (jumps or leaps) won't be as simple. But stay true to the original work as much as possible. Divide into groups of no more than six dancers. Let the first group of dancers mark through their pieces two times in the center of the room, then let the next group of dancers work with the new tempo, and so on until everyone has had a turn. Those off at the side awaiting their turn should do the following:

- Mark through sections of the dance (but don't interfere with those working in the center of the room).
- Listen to the music and visualize choreography at the new tempo.
- Observe while others are reworking their choreography, and learn from their experiences.

Repeat the process two more times so each group of dancers works in the main space a total of three times.

Present the dances individually or, if time is an issue, in groups of two or three.

Group Reflection

Each person should answer the first question.

- While reworking your solo for the new tempo, did you discover anything about your solo that you hadn't noticed before? If yes, what was it?
- Did you notice a significant shift in the performance dynamics (emotions, weight of attack, and so on) for yourself or in others? If yes, describe.

Performance Variation 3

Listen to track 19. It's the same composition, but it's played at a faster tempo than the original. Repeat the same process as in variation 2 to modify the choreography for this new tempo. Some movements will be easy to shorten and condense, and other parts will be more difficult. When everyone is ready to perform, present and discuss the work with the same questions that follow variation 2.

Student Journal 3.4

All handout materials are available on the companion Web site at www.HumanKinetics.com/DanceComposition.

Name _____ Date _____ Class _____

Student Journal 3.4

1. How did your relationship to your movement sequence change over the course of the exercise? (Did you become more conscious of your energy filling space in the slow variation? Did your breathing or focus change when you were working quickly?)

   _____
   _____
   _____
   _____
   _____
   _____

2. Which tempo did you most enjoy working with? Why?

   _____
   _____
   _____
   _____
   _____
   _____

3. Which tempo variation was the most challenging? Why?

   _____
   _____
   _____
   _____
   _____
   _____
   _____

From J. Porter, 2009, *Dance Composition: An Interrelated Arts Approach* (Champaign, IL: Human Kinetics).

Artist Highlight Interview

Parmela Attariwala.
Barry Prophet, photographer. www.pomer-prophet.com.

Parmela Attariwala performs traditional and modern compositions on the viola and violin. She is also a composer and a sonic and movement improviser. Raised in Calgary and now living in Toronto, Parmela holds a BA in music from Indiana University and an MA in ethnomusicology from the School of Oriental and African Studies in London, England. This interview first appeared in the winter 2004 issue of *M(a)Glzone*.

I first met Parmela through her music. At the time I had no idea she danced. Parmela's first CD, *Beauty Enthralled*, was released in 1998. It featured the monumental work "Music for Solo Violin" by the late Harry Somers, and four other compositions by Western composers who have been influenced by Indian music. In an improv section of a class, I introduced my dance students to the opening piece, "La," for violin, tabla, and drones by Robert Rosen. The students loved it. In the spring of 2003 I heard that Parmela was launching her CD *Sapphire Skies* at the Music Gallery in Toronto. At the concert I discovered Parmela was not only a brilliant musician but a very physical performer as well. Several compositions created by Parmela were in collaboration with bharatanatyam dancer Gitanjali Kolanad. In those pieces, Gitanjali wasn't alone when she moved. Parmela danced as well, all the while playing the violin. She played while lying on the floor, traveling across the room with deep lunging steps, and balancing on one foot in a stylized hatha yoga posture. It was sonically and visually exhilarating. Over the years I've had several opportunities to talk with Parmela about her work as a musician, performing artist, and composer.

JP: **When did you start exploring the world of movement and performance music?**

PA: I'll tell you exactly how it happened. In 1996 the Banff Centre (Alberta, Canada) produced a performance art opera called *Kafka's Chimp*. Somebody called and asked me to audition for it. They were looking for a violinist who was interested in modern music. I went in and played the audition. I remember I had a score of contemporary music—it was on paper. I placed it on a music stand, stood behind it, and played. Well, after I finished, they asked me to come out from behind the music stand and play something from memory. I did, and whatever I did from memory was enough to tell them that I had movement energy in my body, and that was what was required for the character of the violinist in the opera.

So that's where it started. That summer I created the role of the violinist and I had to seduce the chimpanzee into humanity. It was crazy: a 90-minute, completely memorized and unconducted opera! All the musicians had character roles and were moving around the stage. I found it extraordinarily liberating to be moving. Before doing that opera, I had had problems with nerves, and working through the opera, somehow the movement alleviated those problems.

JP: **Split focus.**

PA: Yes. I became free with my playing because there was something else to think about besides *Am I doing the right bowing? Am I doing the right fingering?* and all that violin nonsense. A few months after doing the opera, I met bharatanatyam dancer Gitanjali Kolanad. She was looking for someone to help translate Western music for East Indian musicians because of a piece she wanted to choreograph in India, based on Kurt Weil's music. While we were working on that, I mentioned how I was interested in movement, and she said she loves to work with musicians. Well, that was the beginning of our partnership.

Parmela Attariwala and Gitanjali Kolanad.
Barry Prophet, photographer.
www.pomer-prophet.com.

JP: **And how did that evolve?**

PA: I asked Gita to be on my CD-release tour for *Beauty Enthralled* and told her I wanted to do something unusual. So we came up with a piece called "Piercing Embrace." Gita led the movement discovery; I just sat in her studio and Gita would say, "Can you do this? Now try this." And I would try things, all the while pretending I was holding the violin as we explored the different movements. I had to see if I could really do the positions and play the violin at the same time.

JP: **That's what's so amazing watching the two of you work together. To see you perform such a high quality of music while doing a pleading contraction on the floor where you're basically balanced on one hip and your toes. You held that position and kept playing! It was so exciting, very** different from watching a traditional violin soloist, which is a relatively stationary performance experience.

PA: That's interesting. You know, very few of my colleagues in the traditional music world have seen me perform my own work.

JP: **Is that because they don't cross over into new performance styles in the concerts they attend?**

PA: Yes.

JP: **Now when you say "traditional musicians," are you referring to your colleagues in the National Ballet and the Canadian Opera Company orchestras?**

PA: Yes, the ballet. I've done a lot of ballets and they've always been inspiring. I was playing the viola for Karen Kain's farewell tour and didn't have much to play half the time, so whenever I wasn't playing, I was watching her, and it was like seeing music. She was the music when she danced.

JP: **How do you manage the transition from classical to contemporary music?**

PA: I've been playing the traditional stuff for most of my professional life. Contemporary music has been a fairly recent thing, when you consider that I've been playing the violin for 30-some years. I became involved with new music when I returned to Canada about a dozen years ago. I'd done some contemporary music years ago, before I went to Europe, but when I was in Europe contemporary music wasn't happening in the places I was living and with the people I was working with. It wasn't necessary for a musician to have to play contemporary music.

JP: **So when you came back to Canada, you got back into it due to necessity?**

PA: No, no, I did it because I missed it. I felt very confined always playing music from the past, with its own rigidity of how it had to be played, and that added to my performance nerves. For me I need to be completely in a composition when I perform.

JP: **And since you started moving and being physically active in your performances, it's changed the way you work.**

PA: It's a result of having started moving, and, well, even before, with the release of the first CD when I started improvising, that got me into a mind-set of creativity. So now I look at any piece of music, whether it's mine or someone else's, whether it's contemporary or classical, and see it as a piece of creation. In other words, I look at the form as opposed to the technical demands.

I sometimes wonder if I'm perhaps too visually motivated when it comes to sound, because I have always seen music all my life. With every Mozart concerto I ever played, I always had an image in my head of what I wanted the piece to look like if I could visually represent it. There was a sound associated with the visual in my head.

I'm at a point now where I'm interested in creating and expanding the way I create sounds. I'm wondering how I can use my visual sensibilities.

When I watch films, half the time I'm not interested in the dialogue; I'm listening to the soundtrack. Even in my childhood when I watched TV, I listened to the scores. I wanted to be in the L.A. Philharmonic so I could play the TV scores.

JP: **Besides working with Gita, you've worked with other dancers and dance companies. Tell me about your work with Kokoro Dance in Vancouver.**

PA: Oh, my gosh, look! [Lifts her sweater to expose Kokoro Dance T-shirt underneath.]

JP: **(After we stop laughing) How did you get involved with them?**

PA: I became involved with Kokoro through Robert Rosen. He composed "La," the opening track from my first CD. He does a lot of music for Kokoro, and he wanted a live violin or viola and flute to accompany the dancers along with prerecorded tracks he'd done for a composition. We were to play from a written score, as well as watch the dancers, and pick up on their movements and emotions. It was incredible and at times so draining.

JP: **Why was it so draining?**

PA: It was emotionally draining. There was a lot of pain and aggression in their movements. All of the deep human emotions were being portrayed on stage.

JP: **Can you describe the performance style?**

PA: It's butoh-based work. They're all covered in ash, or chalk, and they're basically naked, with loincloths, I think, and they're out there. It's raw, extremely raw human emotion. During rehearsals Robert would say to me, "What you did was great, but can you give me more?" I was always exhausted after the shows.

JP: **When you follow a dancer, it's like following a living score. Instead of the notes being drawn on page, the information is breathing and moving right in front of you. You're feeding off of them and they're feeding off of you.**

PA: I love improv because it forces me to be absolutely in the moment, which is a sensation that composed music and choreographed movement don't always allow one to have. There is a wonderful offshoot of the Association of Improvising Musicians of Toronto called CoexisDance that has monthly workshops and improv performances involving both musicians and dancers. Through CoexisDance, butoh artist Claudia Wittmann and I began working together and discovered a wonderful creative rapport in which we both move and make sound through the performance space. Aesthetically we challenge each other and we've developed a trust that pushes us to physical, emotional, and sonic daring in our performances. We call our duo Zufall—coincidence—one of my favorite German words not only for the overtones of its meaning but for its sound and feel as it is pronounced.

For more information about Parmela Attariwala and her music, go to www.parmela.com.

CHAPTER 4

Texture and Tone Color

Sonic textures are sculptural; they carve the air and delineate space. Tone color is painterly, filling the air with sound. You may think this is a modern music concept, but humans have been experimenting and composing with sonic texture and tone color from the earliest times. Rattles, drums, and gongs have distinct sonic textures—each one affects us viscerally in its own unique way. Bagpipes, for example, were used in battle to frighten the enemy—it's an eerie, almost blood-chilling sound to hear rising up through the mist. By way of contrast, there are the Roman chants (the most familiar is Gregorian) and Tibetan Buddhist mantras designed to be sung on a single pitch, yet they never sound flat or lifeless. In both cases the chanting is full and warm. No two voices have the same tone color, so the air is "painted" with a richness of tonal hues.

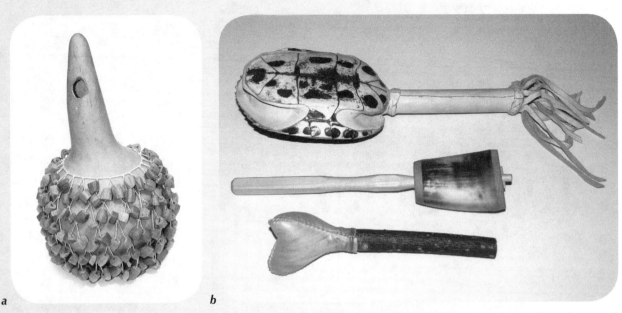

(a) An African gourd rattle and *(b)* Native American rattles made of animal horn, turtle shell, and animal skin.
Barry Prophet, photographer. www.pomer-prophet.com.

Imagine walking barefoot over these textures:

- Marble
- Sandpaper
- Pebbles
- Fur
- Foam
- Hot tar
- Chipped ice
- Broken glass
- Mashed potatoes

The walk changes with each texture from pleasurable to cautious, painful to playful. Textures affect the way we move.

Exercise 4.1 Textural Exploration

Exploring the Visceral Properties of Sound

MUSIC SELECTIONS
Tracks 20, 21, and 22

Exercise 3.1 highlights awareness of the body's internal rhythm (heartbeat and breath). Exercise 4.1 encourages dancers to feel sound through the body's largest organ, the skin.

The use of three CD players (and three copies of the CD) will make the Creation and Presentation element of this exercise more powerful.

Observation

Sonic textures not only sound different; they also feel different. Think of a song or instrumental melody. Imagine listening to it in its original form, then imagine listening to the same piece of music sung by a chorus of caterwauling cats, then again by a chorus of foghorns. Each of those textures creates a distinct physical and emotional response from the listener.

Preparation for Internal Exploration

Create and memorize a repeatable movement pattern focusing on hand movements along the body. Here is an example:

- Left palm travels down left cheek to chin.
- Left palm shifts to right side of neck and continues down right arm and top of right hand.
- Right palm descends along the outside of right thigh. After it has passed the knee, it travels along the inside of the left knee down to the inside of the ankle.
- Left palm touches the outside of left ankle, then both palms travel up either side of the left leg, up either side of the torso, neck, and face, touching the cheeks.
- To repeat the pattern, release the right hand and move the left hand from the left cheek to chin.

The movement pattern will be used in exploring three sonic textures. The musical compositions are the same length, but because the textural qualities are so contrasting, the length of the piece and participants' emotional and physical responses will vary. Performing the same movement sequence for all three compositions deepens awareness of how sonic textures can affect movement.

Internal Exploration

MUSIC SELECTION
Track 20

1. Perform the movement pattern to the first piece of music. Allow the sounds to influence the speed, depth, and flow of movement. Does the music conjure up images or environments? If so, allow them to influence the movement.
2. Continue working the pattern until the music stops, and wait in neutral until the second texture is played.

MUSIC SELECTION
Track 21

3. Move to the second composition. Allow the new sounds to influence the speed and quality of the movement pattern and the internal images.
4. Continue working the pattern until the music stops. Wait in neutral until the third texture is played.

MUSIC SELECTION
Track 22

5. Work with the third music selection and allow the music to influence the speed, quality, and flow of the movements.
6. Continue working the pattern until the music stops. Rest in neutral.

External Exploration

Divide the class into two groups and perform the internal exploration exercise for one another. One group should perform all three variations before sitting down to observe the other group.

Group Reflection

Each of the textures should be described on its own and in relationship to the others. Start the discussion and comparison by responding to these surveys.

- Everyone in the class should contribute one comment for each of the textures, focusing on how to describe them as individual sounds (such as liquid, salty, stinging). Play the first 5 to 10 seconds of the sonic compositions to review the sounds. Do a quick survey to see if there was a texture everyone interpreted the same way or if one texture generated vastly differing responses.
- Compare textures. For example, did a texture slow or speed the movements? Were some textures harder or easier to listen to while moving than while sitting still in the audience? (Some sounds make people squirm, and dancing to the sounds offers release.)

Creation and Presentation

Work in silence with a partner and choreograph a short (no longer than 90-second) duet that meets these requirements:

- Create five ways of physically connecting (work different levels, body parts, weight shifting, and so on).

The author exploring sonic and visual textures with "The Bamboo Quiver" at the Tree Museum.
Barry Prophet, photographer.
www.pomer-prophet.com.

- Make the connections move (shoulder rubs spine, necks intertwine, and so on).
- Have no more than 3 seconds of unconnected movement work at a time.

Present one pair (or, if there are many duets, two or three pairs) at a time. Use the three CD players in the following way:

1. Each CD should be set to one of the three textures.
2. One CD starts, and that sound signals the duet to begin.
3. Another CD with a contrasting or the same textural composition will come on, and the first texture will either fade or continue.
4. A third texture will appear; those manipulating the CDs will explore volumes and textural relationships while the dancers perform their duets.
5. Dancers will hold their final shape to signal that the choreography is finished and the music will fade to finish.
6. Everyone who wishes to should have an opportunity to mix the sound. Each mix should be different. Try all three CDs with the same texture starting at different times, explore silences in between different textures, increase and decrease the volume, and so on.
7. If only one CD is available, ask dancers to perform two times—each time to a different textural composition.

Final Group Reflection

- How did the textures interact with the relationship between dancers?
- Did working with the three CDs challenge individuals' musicality as performers and composers? If yes, describe how.
- Did combining textures create new textures?

Student Journal 4.1

All handout materials are available on the companion Web site at www.HumanKinetics.com/DanceComposition.

Exercise 4.2 Tonal Exploration

Defining Tone Color

MUSIC SELECTION
Tracks 23, 24, and 25

The exercise deepens dancers' understanding of the differences between tone color, note, and pitch.

Track 23 is a short composition containing the same note played at the same pitch *but* with different tone colors. (A wide range of instruments, such as cello, French horn, and gong, can play the same note, from the same octave, but each instrument has a different tone color.)

Track 24 is a short composition containing the same note and same tone color *but* different pitches or levels of frequency. (The notes in the C major scale are C, D, E, F, G, A, B, and C; instruments have ranges anywhere from 2.5 to 5 octaves, allowing many different Cs and Ds on a single instrument.)

Track 25 is a short composition containing the same note *but* different tone color and different pitch. (The piccolo plays the notes at a much higher pitch and a different tone color than the tuba.)

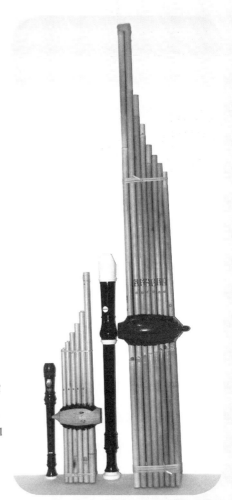

European recorders and Asian Pacific bamboo mouth organs. Instruments are built in a wide range of sizes to cover an extended number of octaves. The smaller recorder in the photograph is 9 inches (23 cm) while the larger cana is 39 inches (1 m) long.

Barry Prophet, photographer. www.pomer-prophet.com.

Observation

Lie on the floor, close your eyes, and listen to the three compositions two times through and observe your responses. Do the compositions relax or irritate you? Do they conjure up vivid images? Don't force a response; just let the sounds wash over you while you observe.

Internal Exploration

Listen to the three compositions two more times while moving. Respond to each of the compositions' unique qualities. The music has challenging aspects—become the music, be moved by the music, and explore the possibilities.

External Exploration

Divide into two groups and watch each other explore the movement potential of the compositions. Continue exploring the sonic relationships of the movement.

Group Reflection

- Each person should comment on the composition he or she felt most strongly about and explain why.

- In a general discussion, describe similarities and differences observed while watching others move through each of the compositions. Were there powerful examples of movements complementing or contrasting the sounds? If yes, describe the effectiveness of each approach.

Creation and Presentation

Divide the class into three or six ensembles with four to seven people per group. Each ensemble will be assigned one of the three compositions (if there are six ensembles, two groups will explore the same composition) and will create a structured movement study for their composition. The choreography shouldn't be too long; the compositions are only 60 seconds long.

Make sure each movement study explores the following elements:

- Explore sounds that have the same pitch, color, or note by repeating an action, and explore how same sounds create tension for contrasting movement.

- Explore sounds that are different in pitch or color by varying that action (different levels, tempo, dramatic expression), and explore how different sounds create tension for repetitive movements.

- Explore spatial relationships between sounds (harmony, discordance, silence) by varying focus, direction, and spatial relationships of movers.

- Keep the movement structure simple; 20 to 25 minutes should be adequate time to create and rehearse the work.

Final Group Reflection

- Have a member of each ensemble describe the group's greatest challenge.
- If more than one ensemble was working with the same composition, were the ideas behind both movement studies the same or different? Which of the ensembles was more powerful and why?

Student Journal 4.2

All handout materials are available on the companion Web site at www.HumanKinetics.com/DanceComposition.

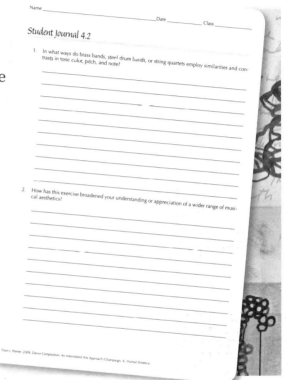

Arts Connection

American composer and instrument maker Harry Partch (1901-1974) explored sonic textures and tonalities in the instruments he made. His work includes the wonderfully named "Cloud Chamber Bowls" (suspended glass gongs), "Boo 1" and "Boo 2" (bamboo marimbas), and "Spoils of War." Partch developed harmonic, microtonal tunings based on mathematical systems and was inspired by many world music traditions (including Polynesian and Balinese instruments and compositional styles and Japanese Noh and Kabuki theater). His book *Genesis of a Music* (Da Capo Press, 1978) is a must-read for anyone interested in the evolution of 20th-century music, experimental tunings, and instrument making. You can learn more about Harry Partch at the Web site www.harrypartch.com.

Exercise 4.3 Found Sound

MUSIC SELECTION
None

Generating One's Own Sound

Drawing on tradition and experimentation, this exercise encourages dancers to explore the sonic potential of simple props and everyday objects.

Observation

Human beings generate sound. We can do it without an extraneous instrument: We make sounds when we breathe, when we walk, and obviously when we talk. What other sounds can we make?

Barry Prophet and Janice Pomer perform "Site and Sound" at New Adventures in Sound Art Festival. "Site and Sound" playfully explores the sonic and visual potential of plastic hose pipes, wired tin cans, wooden sticks, metal discs, and other found sounds.

Stefan Rose, photographer.
www.townsendretraced.ca.

Internal Exploration

There are numerous acoustic sound-generating devices that are not commonly associated with sound or music in the studio. Look around the studio. There may be books, chairs, shoes, keys, the wall, and other objects that generate sound.

1. When the facilitator calls out "Go!", find a sound-generating object and explore its sonic potential. There might not be enough objects in the room for everyone. If that's the case, let the body become an instrument. Explore as wide a range of body-generated sounds as possible. (For example, you already know how to speak, so avoid words but try clicks, pops, gurgling, and other vocal sounds. Or contract and expand your abdomen and play it like a drum—listen to the differences as the surface goes from concave to convex.)
2. After 60 seconds, the facilitator will call out, "Change." Everyone must move to another object and explore it for 60 seconds.
3. There'll be two more explorations of 60 seconds in length. During these quick explorations, try to work with a range of objects: small, large, wearable, structural (such as a floor, a door, and a wall).

External Exploration

Repeat the exercise with half of the class moving and generating sound while the other half watches. After both groups have observed the activity, sit down and discuss and reflect.

Group Reflection

Compile a list of all of the objects (not body parts) used in the exercise, then conduct a survey of each object. Ask everyone who used that object (or something close to it) to demonstrate one of the ways he or she used it.

- Were certain objects easier or harder to generate sound with?
- Were any of the sounds surprisingly melodic or surprising in other ways?
- Did everyone use hands to animate the sounds, or did you find other ways to move the object?

Creation and Presentation

Think of all the acoustic sound-generating objects (but not actual instruments) we interact with every day. (For this exercise, radios, MP3 players, and televisions aren't applicable; they are electronic or battery operated, not acoustic. Unfortunately that means great sound generators such as food blenders, hair dryers, and electric drills can't be used, either.)

Make lists of some of the more common sonic generators found in these environments:

- Nature
- Office
- Toy store
- Kitchen

Select one or two of those items or another acoustic sonic generator and create a 2- to 3-minute solo movement and sound piece. There will be no musical accompaniment other than sounds generated by the movement, and the sounds mustn't be vocalizations.

Being the dancer and musician isn't an unusual combination. Traditional dancers from wear the world employ this skill. Think of all the dance forms in which the dancers wear leg or ankle bells, such as classical East Indian dances, traditional English Morris dances, and dances in many Native American cultures. Flamenco dancers use percussive hand castanets, Inuit drum dancers move with large frame drums, and Korean drum dancers play complex polyrhythms on double-headed drums. While dancing, they swing their heads, animating long ribbonlike streamers on their hats called Sangmo, creating smooth, swooping circles overhead. If you're a clogger or tap dancer, this assignment is a logical extension to the metal taps on your shoes.

The sound-generating "instrument" can be large or small, natural or manmade. Work with no more than two different items, but use any quantity of those items

The empty shells on this traditional African dance rattle belt generate loud, crisp sounds when the dancer moves.
Barry Prophet, photographer. www.pomer-prophet.com.

(such as 1,000 paper clips and 1 rake). Have fun, cover the floor with stuff, roll over objects, and kick, bump, and thump things. Test several objects to find the right sonic mix. Forget what the object's normally used for—now it's a musical instrument and dance partner.

Preparation

Much of the work for this exercise will be done outside of class. Many of the found sound solos will require setup and strike time. The facilitator will need to know everyone's plans to create a timetable for the performance.

To help things run smoothly, there will be a deadline for students to complete the following tasks:

- Write a brief artist's statement about the selected sonic objects and the sound–movement relationships explored in the choreography.
- Include the amount of setup or strike time required. For example, if many water-filled bowls need to be placed on the floor, it will be necessary to set them, strike them, and possibly mop the floor afterward. Some materials (such as rocks or nails) might harm the floor. Discuss safety strategies with the facilitator to find ways to prevent causing damage. Choreography requiring a large amount of cleanup time should be scheduled last in the day's viewing.

Safety Note

Work carefully and incorporate wearing protective clothing and safety gear during this exercise. Shoes, gloves, earplugs, and safety glasses might be necessary, depending on the objects employed. Don't take chances. Dance safely.

Follow a performance schedule of no more than seven people to present each day. Each performance day, three or four dancers not presenting will be required to assist with the setup and strike. After all of the performances for the day have been presented, discuss the work.

Final Group Reflection (For Each Day of Presentations)

Ask each dancer who presented to read his or her artistic statement outlining the reasons for selecting the found sound objects. (If there are people who selected the same or similar objects, it's interesting to learn whether their reasons for selecting it were the same.) After hearing the statements, discuss the pieces.

- Did the choreography fulfill the sound–movement relationship outlined in the artist statement? If yes, how? If no, what was lacking and how could it be improved?
- Did the choreography exceed the choreographer's original expectations? If yes, give examples.

Student Journal 4.3

All handout materials are available on the companion Web site at www.HumanKinetics.com/DanceComposition.

Arts Connections

Stomp, the successful "found sound" percussion and movement company, was created in 1991 by Luke Cresswell and Steve McNicholas, whose roots are in street theater, music, and the staging of large outdoor events. Since its formation, Stomp has toured the world amazing audiences with its gritty movements and rhythms created with boxes, garbage cans, and other articles of "street junk." Cresswell and McNicholas have also created the *Lost and Found Orchestra*, which premiered in 2007 in Brighton, England, and has appeared at the Sydney Opera House, Australia. For more information on Stomp, go to www.stomponline.com.

Bart Hopkins is the author of numerous books on making "found sound" instruments. He has worked with experimental tunings and instruments for over 20 years, and for many years he published *Experimental Musical Instruments*, a journal dedicated to unusual instruments and sound-generating devices. His Web site, www.windworld.com, contains information on making unusual instruments and purchasing books, CDs, tapes, and catalogs featuring eccentric instruments. The site also has links to other sites of interest.

Exercise 4.4 Turn Your Radio On

Compositional Exploration With Radios

MUSIC SELECTION
Track 26

MATERIALS: Four radios

This exercise continues to develop dancers' awareness of movement and musical potential of mundane actions and sounds.

In modern dance, it's not uncommon to see ordinary movements integrated into the technique. In the 20th century, choreographers challenged our perception of dance in many ways; one way is the inclusion of mundane actions and gestures (such as sitting in chairs, twitching, and scratching) into dancers' movement vocabulary. While modern dance pioneers were creating new movement lexicons, 20th-century musicians were exploring the sonic potential of noninstrumental objects. Musique concrete (sound art created by manipulating recorded music and electronic and acoustic sounds) dates back to post–World War II. The tape recorder was a wartime invention; it made recording and editing accessible, and experimental musicians were quick to see its creative potential.

Observation

Think back to this morning: waking up, getting out of bed, washing up, dressing, and grabbing something to eat. What sounds accompanied the actions? Most likely the majority of sounds were directly related to the actions (buzz of the alarm, water from the shower), but there were also sounds that were not related to actions (garbage truck, neighbor's dog barking). Take a few minutes to retrace today sonically and visually until arriving here in the studio.

Internal Exploration

MUSIC SELECTION
Track 26

Traditionally, dancers and choreographers interact with and interpret the music they move to, but is that always necessary? Since unrelated sounds and actions happily coexist in real life, it makes sense that those relationships are explored in art.

Play track 26 and improvise with the following elements:

- Technical stationary and locomotor (across-the-floor) combinations from various dance forms
- Gestures such as rubbing your eyes and shrugging
- Daily activities such as household chores, sports, and leisure pursuits

Explore the last two elements fully. Find ways to make those actions as versatile as the technical vocabulary.

External Exploration

MATERIALS: Four radios

Repeat the exercise with a quarter of the class presenting while the others observe. Use these four variations:

1. The first group uses the same mixture of movement elements as in the original exploration.
2. The second group explores the movement potential of gestures only.
3. The third group explores ways to connect and disconnect with the sonic accompaniment using only technical dance vocabulary.
4. The fourth group explores the potential of movements from daily activities.

Those working with variations 2 and 4 should manipulate their actions by changing the tempo and textural, directional, spatial, and emotional qualities throughout the exploration.

Note

Instead of playing the same music track for each of the variations, create original sonic accompaniment by using radios. Volunteers from the observing groups can compose a score by roaming up and down the dial, settling on a station, increasing and decreasing volume, and so on. A different ensemble of radio volunteers should play for each presenting group. Those playing the radios should strive to make their sonic accompaniment different from any of the others by applying compositional elements examined in the earlier exercises.

Group Reflection

Composer Edgard Varèse said, "Music is organized sound." Do a show-of-hands survey to see who agrees or disagrees with that statement. Think back to the radio accompaniments and identify specific moments when these compositional elements were most prevalent:

- Rhythmic patterns
- Tempo changes
- Textural and tonal variations
- Harmonic elements

Can we rephrase Varèse's statement to "Dance is organized actions"? Survey the class to see who agrees or disagrees with that statement and discuss. In the four variations, technical and nontechnical movement were explored. Did only the technical dance contain the following elements?

- Dynamic exploration of motion and stillness
- Interesting use of spatial relationships
- Complementary and contrasting tempos and rhythms
- Dramatic expression

Or did all of the variations contain these choreographic elements? Is it the action, the intent, or a combination of both that makes a dance?

Creation and Presentation

Fifty years ago, few people owned tape recorders. Now almost everyone has some form of personal recording device. Use whatever recording technology is available to create a 45- to 60-second sonic composition containing a mix of voice, precomposed music, atmospheric sounds, and sonic textures. You don't need to be high-tech to do this; a telephone answering machine will do the job. Work with available technology.

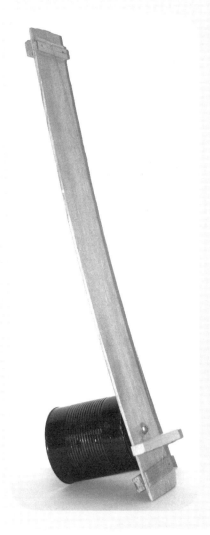

Modern materials can be used to recreate new versions of old instruments. Musician and instrument maker Ben Grossman fashioned this single string musical bow using a tin can and guitar string instead of the traditional gourd and animal gut.

Barry Prophet, photographer. www.pomer-prophet.com.

1. Listen to all the sound compositions.
2. Divide into groups of three or four. Each group will develop a playing strategy for their compositions (all at the same time, pulsing in and out, and so on) to accompany another group's movement exploration. This should take no more than 3 minutes.
3. One group will be at the playback machines, and another group will go into the performance area. The remaining groups will be the audience. Those in the performance area will improvise using the same vocabulary as in the internal and external observations: technical combinations from various dance forms, gestures, and daily activities.
4. Dancers may or may not wish to be affected by the sonic accompaniment. Dancing and moving without any apparent connection to the music can be as effective a performance tool as moving dramatically or sympathetically with it.

Final Group Reflection

Compile a list of all the sounds used in the compositions.

- If some of the compositions contained a unique compilation of sounds, ask the creators to describe their compositional process.
- What was the most challenging aspect of this exercise? Why?

Student Journal 4.4

All handout materials are available on the companion Web site at www.HumanKinetics.com/DanceComposition.

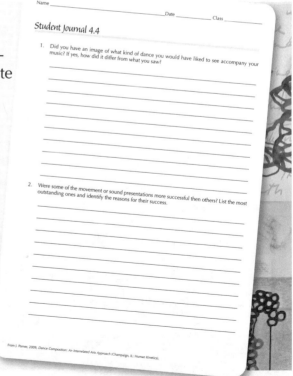

Arts Connection

In 1960, John Cage composed "Cartridge Music" for Merce Cunningham's choreography of "Changing Steps." The choreography was "indeterminate," meaning the performance could be performed for any length of time, in any space, and by any number of dancers. The composition was performed on old phonograph cartridges and amplified small objects inserted into the cartridges (pipe cleaners, wires, feathers, and Slinkies). Much has been written about the individual achievements of John Cage and Merce Cunningham and their partnership. Their masterworks have been documented in volumes of books, recordings, and videos. Respected writer and electro-acoustic composer Richard Kostelanetz has edited and written books on both artists. Go to www.merce.org and www.johncage.info.

Culminating Exercise for Dance and Music

This duet will be marked using the rubrics and self-evaluation forms found on the companion Web site. As the culminating exercise for part 2, you are expected to incorporate ideas explored in the preceding exercises of this section. Unlike the culminating exercise for part 1, this exercise involves working with a partner. Each person's ideas and abilities should support the others. Respect is the key to a successful partnership. You need not have the same aesthetics to make a partnership work. Some of the best partnerships work because there are tensions, but if difficulties in the partnership arise, talk to the facilitator before they become insurmountable.

Music and Movement Partnership

MUSIC SELECTION
Tracks 35 through 73

A compositional and choreographic duet

Cocreate a computer-assisted sonic composition and use the composition as a foundation for a dance duet.

The final assignment in this section is to cocreate an original composition using computer-assisted music. Work with a partner to create a 2- to 3-minute sonic composition, and choreograph a duet to be performed with the score. Those with experience with computer software or computer music should be teamed with those who are less skilled, but the assignment is friendly to everyone regardless of computer skills.

The companion Web site contains a manual (written by Barry Prophet, who composed all of the music on the CD) for using the freeware music software Audacity. Freeware is a term used for any computer software freely downloadable from a Web site. Just follow these steps:

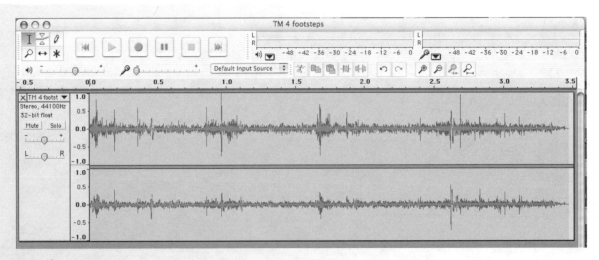

Sound waves.
Barry Prophet, photographer. www.pomer-prophet.com.

1. Go to the companion Web site and follow the directions for downloading the Audacity software and instruction manual.
2. Tracks 35-72 on the CD contain your sound library.
3. Save the sound library as described in the manual.
4. Familiarize yourself with Audacity by completing the instructional exercise.
5. Create a 2- to 3-minute composition employing the music elements explored in this section:
    - Spatial relationships
        - Between sounds and silences to create rhythms
        - Between individual notes to create harmonies
    - Tempo (rhythm)
        - The speed at which music is played
        - Rhythmic patterns
    - Pitch: the octave placement (high, medium, low) of a note
    - Tone color: the note's unique resonance or flavor
    - Textures: the emotional or dynamic quality of a sound
6. Complete the composition and then choreograph the duet (or develop the music and the dance at the same time).
7. After the dance and the music are set, write a brief artistic statement (100 to 150 words) explaining music and choreographic choices. The artistic statement may cover the following material:
    - What specific theme, environment, or idea is being explored?
    - What sounds or movements are being employed to convey this theme?
    - Does some of the dance visually illustrate musical elements (bodies working closely while sounds are tightly overlapping)?
    - Are there areas in which the dance and musical elements purposefully work against each other? If yes, why?

This project may take several weeks to complete. The facilitator will set a performance schedule. It's best to divide the presentations over 2 or 3 days. Each performance session should feature four or five pieces followed by a group discussion of the work. Artistic statements should be printed out and ready for distribution to the audience before presenting.

Final Group Reflection (End of Each Performance Day)

Audience members will have had time to read the artists' statements before viewing the dances.

- What was the most successful element in the music?
- What was the most successful element in the dance?
- Did the statement add to the appreciation of the performance? If yes, describe how.

Self-Evaluation for Dance and Music

All handout materials are available on the companion Web site at www.HumanKinetics.com/DanceComposition.

Rubric for Culminating Exercise for Dance and Music

All handout materials are available on the companion Web site at www.HumanKinetics.com/DanceComposition.

Artist Highlight Interview

Nejla Yatkin performing "After."
Astrid Riecken/The Washington Times.

Nejla Yatkin is an award-winning dancer and choreographer and was recognized by *Dance Magazine* as one of the "Top 25 Dancers to Watch" in 2005. She received her master's degree in dance and choreography from Die Etage, the performing arts academy in Berlin, Germany. Currently based in Washington, DC, Nejla tours internationally and since 2001 is an associate professor of dance at the University of Maryland, College Park.

I first interviewed Nejla in 2003 at Toronto's Fringe Festival of Independent Dance Artists (fFIDA) after a performance of her magnificent solo "After." The first half of this interview is an excerpt of a longer piece that originally appeared in the fall 2003 issue of *M(a)GIzone*.

JP: **You created the choreography and the sound design for your piece. The score is a blend of voice, environmental sounds, and symphonic music. Tell me about the genesis of the dance and how you constructed the score.**

NY: The idea started after September 11, and that's why the piece is called "After." The event of September 11 was so present. Every night you saw it in the media and it was haunting. When you turned on the television you'd see these images over and over again. The idea of being haunted by one event was the idea of the piece.

I was on tour at the time that I started working on the piece. I toured six countries in Eastern Europe. While on tour I talked to artists and asked them about loss and what they would say to someone in their last few minutes. I recorded everything they said on video. I was very aware of talking to people with different accents because the voices have rhythms and I wanted to integrate that into the composition to make the dance more approachable to audiences in various countries.

When I was going through dance images, I was hearing sounds I wanted to have playing for certain parts in the dance. I knew the first movement needed a fast, overwhelming drum section, but I didn't want to have drums or a traditional rhythm that goes continuously. I wanted to have a feeling of disconnection and fragmentation, so you're hearing it sometimes, but not always. The next section was to play with the voices, to put them in a way that makes a musical climax, but with voice. And the watery sound that you heard—it wasn't really water; it was breathing. We taped different kinds of breathing in the studio and we mixed it together and it sounded like water. There were also different sounds that the people I interviewed made. We exaggerated those sounds and echoed them. And there was a poem section, by Pablo Neruda. I recorded that several times at different volumes and mixed it with the breathing. The final was an excerpt of Henryk Górecki's Symphony No. 3. He composed it soon after World War II, and the work was first performed in September 1946 in a little church. I used the final 3 minutes of it, and the song that she's singing is about a mother who yearns for her lost son. The text, a prayer, was found written on the wall in a concentration camp.

JP: **You're very involved in designing your own scores. Is this something you've been doing for a long time?**

NY: No, I just started. This is the first time. Normally I just go to the craziest section of the music store and buy CDs. I listen to funky music and avant-garde music, and sometimes I find something and sometimes I don't. This time it was a commission, and I wanted music created specially for this piece. I was hearing the music in my head. Usually I hear other people's music and create to it, but this time I had the structure for the dance and I was hearing the music inside of me.

JP: **Do you think you will continue to create your own scores?**

NY: Oh, yes. It's very interesting. I like the process very much. The outcomes are so unique and surprising. You can build the dance and make it whole—from its core outward. By creating with different sounds and words, you make your dance rounder, fuller; they're not separate. It's different from when you take a piece of music from somewhere else and make a dance to go with it. When you create your own score, when you're involved in both the sound and the movement, it's fuller and more integrated.

Nejla Yatkin.
Astrid Riecken/The Washington Times.

We reconnected by phone in fall 2006.

JP: **"After" was an international success. Since then, have you continued exploring creative musical elements for dance?**

NY: After I completed "After," I started working with jazz musicians, and that was a very different challenge. I'd choreographed a dance with movements at a certain tempo in mind, but we'd rehearse with the musicians only once a week. Because the musicians were used to playing freely, it was hard for them to keep one strict tempo. At first the dancers found it very difficult to work with the timing changes, but in the performances it all came together. During the rehearsals we struggled with the different tempos. In each rehearsal the musicians felt the music differently, and that was fine for them because their score was open and free, but the dancers had set choreography and the fluctuation in tempo is challenging.

JP: **So this was an ensemble piece?**

NY: Yes, it's called "Gaia Rising." The piece was about migration, moving from one place to another. It explores the questions "What do you take with you?" and "What do you leave behind?" The jazz music was the background for it, and jazz music itself migrated from one place to another and was influenced by different cultures.

JP: **Over the course of the rehearsals, did the dancers start to work more like the musicians, listening to each other, playing with the tempo shifts, and responding to each other's movements?**

NY: They got so in tune with it that by the performance they were giving each other cues on when to start and how to move, and they played with spatial relationships.

JP: **There's a wonderful correlation to the space between notes and the space between dancers. How did that influence the choreography?**

NY: The dancers took ownership of the choreography. When dancers interact with each other and the music, then they've made the movement their own. You have dialogue with the musicians and with the dancers and the space. That's three levels, and then there's your internal dialogue of what you need to do and why.

JP: **"Gaia Rising" was an ensemble work for dancers and musicians. Now you're focusing on solo dance accompanied by a solo musician in your newest piece titled "Solo," choreographed to J.S. Bach's Cello Suites. What is it about the music that inspired you to choose it?**

NY: It's such a beautiful composition, very mathematical and structured, yet full of variations and freedom and infinite possibilities. At first I read a lot about the *Cello Suites*, and from that research I realized nobody really knows exactly how they're supposed to be played. Musicians have interpreted the pieces many ways, and there's just so much potential for variations in the music that I decided I would focus my choreography on the structure of the music. So, in a sense, I built the dance from the inside and let the emotional context grow out of that.

JP: Is that how you sensitize yourself to sound from the inside out?

NY: I've always had a sense of space, of inside and outside. I think we're influenced by sound. We take it inward, inside ourselves, and create our own physical response. It's an instantaneous exchange and it happens more clearly when you work with live musicians, but there's always an energy exchange between sound energy and movement energy. You take the sound in, digest it in your system, and put it out there in a split second. You have to be aware of your surroundings, your external and internal space, the sounds around you, and the sounds inside you.

For more information about Nejla Yatkin, go to her Web site www.ny2dance.com.

PART III

Dance and the Dramatic and Literary Arts

A good story goes a long way. Read any of Joseph Campbell's books exploring the synchronicity of world mythology, and you'll see how similar humanity's ancient myths and legends are. The same is true when you read or listen to folktales from around the world. Common themes, lessons, and characters are found in Native American, African, Asian, Arctic, Indo-Pacific, and European folktales. These tales weren't merely told for entertainment; they were educational vehicles. Through oral story traditions, we teach children rules to live by, and many of those simple folktales became the foundation for the great classic poems, novels, and theatrical works of the world.

Denise Fujiwara performing "Heroic Garb," choreographed by Tedd Robinson.
John Lauener, photographer. www.jlphoto.ca.

The first known novel is *Story of Sinuhe*. It was written in Egypt more than 3,500 years ago. At that time the Egyptians used an alphabet of 24 signs, wrote on papyrus, and had built libraries. Halfway around the world, China was experiencing its first of seven periods of classical literature, and 500 years later (approximately 3,000 years ago) they had created a dictionary containing 40,000 characters. One thousand years later, in 496 B.C., Sophocles, one of ancient Greece's most popular playwrights, was born. His plays have lost none of their power and relevance over the centuries and are still performed frequently around the world.

Dance is relatively new to written notation. In recent times, video and film have been effective in preserving choreography, but dancers have preserved traditional and classical dances over centuries in the same process as the old storytellers: orally transmitting dances from one generation to another. With each telling, the dance and the story deepen, and each dance artist brings new wisdom and insight to the dance.

Whether we're dancing the story of Hunaman the Monkey King from the Mahabharata or re-creating a role for a contemporary multimedia performance piece, dancers are dramatic artists expressing ideas and emotions. Even when we aren't trying to convey emotions, we're communicating. The very act of stepping out on a stage says something. When we turn our heads or raise our arms we say something. We cannot *not* communicate.

The exercises in part III develop the following skills:

Emotional depth

Commitment to character

Performance dynamics

Vocal skills

Silent and spoken soliloquies and monologues

CHAPTER 5

Emotions and Character

Rarely are the characters in folktales emotionally complex or highly developed. Many of the characters are stereotypical: innocent child, wise elder, cruel adult in position of power, and so on. The characters conform to a specific set of attitudes—we are guileless when we are young, we acquire wisdom with age—that contains a great deal of truth but is by no means absolute. What makes the characters come alive is the listener. As we listen to a folktale, our inner voices project our own emotions and experiences into the characters and situations. It's that same inner voice that performers draw on to enliven and empower the characters they portray on stage or film.

Exercise 5.1 Emotional Exploration

Increasing Emotional Dynamics

MUSIC SELECTION
Tracks 27 through 33

This exercise encourages exploration of emotional range and the discovery of emotional impulses.

Actors develop emotional range just as dancers strive to increase their physical range. Dance requires a balance of strength and flexibility of the body, whereas acting demands emotional flexibility and disciplined control of one's emotional palette. Just as a visual artist creates a grayscale by systematically increasing the density of a color, an actor must be able to express degrees of emotional intensity.

Observation

Think of emotions as energized motions, or to borrow from Einstein's most famous equation, E + motion = emotion. Whether we look at it artistically or scientifically, it's a simple fact: emotions move us. Print up the student journal handout for this exercise and, on your own, read through the list of examples of emotions and how they move us:

- Pace with worry.
- Stammer with indecision.
- Nerves shatter.

Storyteller, dancer, and musician Emerita Emerencia performing in a dance Immersion Showcase Presentation in 2003.
David Hou, photographer. www.davidhou.com.

- Bubble with excitement.
- Squirm with embarrassment.
- Float with happiness.
- Shake with glee.

The list is composed of seven relatively common emotions that we've all experienced.

Take another 2 minutes to read the list again. This time, after each emotional movement phrase, internalize the image, both the feeling and the physical impulse. Taste each emotion and its corresponding physical sensation, even the uncomfortable ones.

There may be other ways in which these emotions can move us. The physical actions these emotions are associated with in the list are by no means exclusive. Write personal, alternative responses beside the suggested ones; there'll be an opportunity to compare them with others' responses during the group reflection.

Internal Exploration

Play the seven compositions three times. Respond improvisationally to each composition. There's no "right" action or emotion; just move in response to the sounds. Avoid acting like a person feeling the emotion—instead try to embody the emotion itself. For example, the emotion anger can be raw, burning, and consuming. Anger boils like hot lava and erupts like a volcano. Anger can also

MUSIC SELECTION
Tracks 27 through 33

Student Journal 5.1a

All handout materials are available on the companion Web site at www.HumanKinetics.com/DanceComposition.

smolder and fester. It can bore inward or slash outward. No emotion is one-dimensional. Listen to the music and the physical impulses within.

External Exploration

Repeat the internal exploration exercise with half of the class observing while the other half works.

Group Reflection

- Did everyone respond with similar emotions and movements to the sounds? If not, identify which sounds resulted in a wide range of responses and discuss the various interpretations.
- How many wrote alternative responses beside any of the emotions on the list before participating in the movement portion of the exercise? Create a list of alternative responses and survey the class to see whether any of those responses are more prevalent than those in the original list.
- Which of the compositions created the strongest emotional environments? Discuss possible reasons for this. (The shape of the composition, the sonic textures were most compelling, it was reminiscent of something very familiar, and so on.)

As a class, select three of the compositions for the class to continue working with in the Creation and Presentation section of the exercise.

Creation and Presentation

MUSIC SELECTION
Three of the compositions selected at the end of the group reflection

The three compositions selected at the end of the previous discussion will be the foundation for several structured improvisational choreographic works. Divide the class into three groups: One third of the class will perform the choreographic structure while the rest of the class watches. Everyone will work with each of the musical compositions. Presentation of the structured improvisations should be organized in the following manner:

1. Let group A perform the choreographic structure with the first composition, followed by group B's and C's performances.
2. Afterward, group B should start with the second composition, followed by group C, and then group A.
3. Continue the pattern—group C leads with the third composition, then group A, and then group B.

Each group follows the same improvised choreographic structure:

1. Everyone starts in parallel position (facing any direction).
2. When the music begins, maintain parallel position for several deep breaths.
3. During the opening breaths, each performer will connect with the music internally and emotionally (individuals may respond to the composition differently from the others in their group). This exercise isn't about inter-

preting music the same way as everyone else; it's about listening and responding to internal impulses physically and emotionally.

4. After the opening breaths, begin to move in one of two ways:
   - With large, full-bodied actions that travel across the room.
   - With very small isolations limited to one area of the body.

5. Both the large and small movements originate from a physical and emotional response to the musical composition.

6. During the remaining length of the music, each person's movements must evolve in one of two ways:
   - Increase from small isolation to large and full-body movements.
   - Decrease from full-body movements to small isolation.

7. When the music stops, freeze, take several deep breaths, then slowly "melt" back into parallel position.

8. Each group should perform this improvised choreographic structure to all three of the selected compositions before discussing the experience.

9. To make the experience more potent from a choreographic standpoint, make sure groups explore these variations:
   - Half of the group starts with large movements and the other half starts with small actions.
   - One person starts with small isolations; the rest start with large.
   - One person starts with large; the rest start with small.

Student Journal 5.1b

All handout materials are available on the companion Web site at www.HumanKinetics.com/DanceComposition.

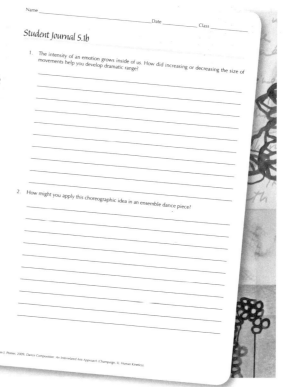

Final Group Reflection

- When you were performing, did you find yourself approaching the limit of large or small movements before the music finished? If yes, did you rely on internal or emotional intensity to help continue the momentum of increasing or decreasing your actions, or did you employ a different strategy?
- How did the number of dancers moving from large to small or small to large affect the dynamics of the exercise?
- Besides the balance of dancers working large versus small, identify other elements that made the choreographic structure interesting.

Arts Connections

Eugène Ionesco's 1959 play *Les Rhinocéros* is a classic of absurdist theater. The play employs a variation of one against many to explore consensual reality. Berenger (the protagonist) and others in the town watch as those around them change into rhinoceroses. A debate ensues about what to do about the wild beasts running through the town, but as more and more people make the shift from human to rhinoceros, the question of what is acceptable and what is not becomes less clear. At the end, Berenger is the only one untouched by the metamorphosis. He alone remains human, but human is no longer "normal." The consensus of the majority has shifted and he is the outsider. The Web site www.ionesco.org (click on the British flag for English text) has more information about the play *Les Rhinocéros* and links to sites about Eugène Ionesco's life, his other literary works, and Theatre of the Absurd.

Theater has always been a forum for exploring the human condition. Whether in ancient times (classic Greek drama) or modern-day plays, theater takes a hard look at society and its morals and ethics. Theater has helped change the world. The Market Theatre of Johannesburg, South Africa (founded by writer and director Barney Simon and producer and administrator Mannie Manim), began in 1974 as an independent nonracial theater at a time when the country was gripped by apartheid. The company produced works by international playwrights and helped develop the works of many South African playwrights. Market Theatre brought outside voices to South Africa and helped South Africans tell their stories to the world. For more information on the Market Theatre, go to www.markettheatre.co.za.

Exercise 5.2 Character Discovery

A Strategy for Character Development

MUSIC SELECTION

Tracks 15, 16, or other atmospheric pieces; facilitator will talk through the imaging text

The exercise builds on the previous exercise. Characters are explored through internal impulse and imagery.

Everyone is unique. When we portray a character, whether in dance, theater, or literature, we need to understand the character from within. We need to listen to internal impulses of action, emotion, and thought—not our own but of the character we've become.

Observation

Imagine being someone else, someone quite different in age and occupation. To find that someone, visualize an environment that by its nature attracts a variety of people: train station, airport, supermarket, park, playground, and so on. Roam through the crowds. There might be a child playing with a toy, an excited traveler, or an executive burdened with files and documents. Choose someone to explore. It might be a person who resembles an acquaintance, or someone completely unfamiliar. Stay connected to that character throughout the exercise.

Internal Exploration

Step 1

Note to Facilitator

Ask everyone to stand in parallel position at least three arm lengths away from others. They should close their eyes and mentally focus on the character chosen for this study. After a minute or two of visualization, read the following text. There needs to be time for everyone to internalize the process so speak slowly, and allow time to pass between each step.

Imaging Text

1. Visualize the place the character was first seen—perhaps an object that comes to view with the character.
2. Concentrate on that place or object. See it in your mind's eye.
3. Concentrate on the character. Visualize him or her.
4. Allow internal awareness of the character to increase with every breath.
5. Let the image fill your lungs when you inhale; when you exhale, let details of the character extend into your limbs and permeate your entire being.

6. As awareness of the character fills you, notice how you respond physically. Are you becoming lighter or heavier, straighter or stooped, more tense or relaxed, outgoing or inward?

7. Observe these physical responses and let them evolve; let them change your appearance. Allow your spine to follow the impulse to lengthen, twist, or round. Allow your hands to clench or hang limp, your feet to turn in or out, your weight to shift.

8. Let yourself move. Follow your first impulse. Don't edit. Walk, run, shuffle, or kick.

9. Stay focused on the character's physical impulses. Let the impulses grow and develop.

10. Become the person for whom these impulses are essential; become the person whose inner core is driven by these physical actions and desires, fears, or urges.

11. You may find your character needs moments of rest. Stillness is fine, but stay in character.

12. Keep your thinking, feeling, and breathing in character. Be in the place where your character is, not in the studio.

13. If your character is hungry, eat. If your character is sleepy, sleep. Do everything in character. Follow the character's impulses. Become someone other than who you are.

Note to Facilitator

Allow dancers to continue working for 5 more minutes, then ask everyone to find a stillness and then slowly release the character.

Step 2

MUSIC SELECTION

Track 15, 16, or other atmospheric pieces

Work with a chair. If the class is large, it might make sense to bring in half the number of chairs and ask people to share so the chairs don't clutter the space.

Create a dramatic movement or dance sequence based on the character. Allow the dramatic movement to be flavored by technical dance expertise. In each character, this blending of skills will manifest differently, but each dramatic movement or dance sequence must have the following elements:

- Reach
- Turn
- Travel forward
- Sit
- The ability to be repeated in full or in part, with different timings and in different sequential order

The music selection will be played four times (if sharing a chair, work with it two of the four times and continue to work the other times without the chair).

External Exploration

MUSIC SELECTION
Track 15, 16, or other atmospheric pieces

Place six chairs in the performance area. The chairs may be in any arrangement. In fact, one element of this structured improvisation is to rearrange the chairs for each ensemble. Chairs can be set to re-create a bus or subway, an airport, or a hospital waiting area, or they can be randomly scattered throughout the performance area.

Ensembles of five or six will work at a time. Don't discuss characters or movement sequences beforehand. Ensemble members will enter the performance area and do the following:

1. Find a spot and either stand or sit. Take 10 seconds in silence to get into character.
2. Move when the music comes on, or wait. Someone will be the first to move, someone will be the last. There's no pressure to be either.
3. While moving, stay in character, but also be peripherally aware of others.
4. Perform the reach, turn, travel forward, and sit movement as a complete sequence or in parts—as bests fits the activity on stage. For example, a character may be uncomfortable sitting near others, so perhaps the sit element is omitted. Or a character feels extremely needy and keeps reaching out to others, so much so that the reach movement is repeated over and over and the other movements are relegated to a minor role.

Group Reflection

Everyone should share a personal observation about his or her character (how each person chose it, what he or she discovered about it, and so on). Afterward, discuss the external observation.

- In general, was the structure successful? If yes, why? If no, why not?
- Did any of the ensembles work more successfully than others? If yes, identify the reasons why. Was it the combination of character types, the pattern of the chairs, the emotional conviction of the performances?

Creation and Presentation

MUSIC SELECTION
Any atmospheric composition from the CD or work in silence

Stay in the same groups. Originally chance played a role in choosing who worked with whom and the placement of the chairs. Now take control over chair placement and music selection, spend time discussing physical and emotional relationships between characters, and develop performance strategies.

Get to know each other's characters. Start with a quick survey and answer the following questions:

- How many explored a character that was older or younger than themselves?
- Is the character more of an introvert or extrovert?
- Is there a simple or obvious reason for this introverted or extroverted behavior?
- What word best describes the character's fundamental makeup (nervous, curious, smug, worried, blasé, sympathetic, and so on)?

Use the information from this simple survey and other knowledge acquired from performing the original structure (for example, some characters may reach out in the same way—can that be used dramatically?) to construct a more specific choreographic structure that will allow for improvisational elements. Ensembles should do the following:

- Establish chair placement.
- Select the music (silence or any track on the accompanying CD).
- Establish an opening preset and order of entry so that each character is introduced and established to the audience. (There won't be time to choreograph solos—all movements other than the structure are improvised.)
- Assign characters to work with (or against) each other for impromptu duets or trios within the ensemble.
- Set a culminating sequence of events.
- Establish a finishing position.

Take 20 minutes to establish the new structure; afterward each ensemble will present, and then the class will discuss the work.

Final Group Reflection

The pieces were improvisational but had a more personalized structure because of the extra planning time and greater understanding that ensemble members had of each other's characters.

How did planning the chair setup and the knowledge of other characters help to

- give the ensemble a physical place to work from,
- give individuals emotional pathways for exploring and communicating with each other, and
- give the audience a more cohesive experience?

The more dancers know about their characters, the more focused their performance choices become. This isn't just true with dramatic characters; the same holds true while dancing abstract shapes and textures. As dancers, we always need to know what we are and how the choreographer wants us to relate to others on the stage even when the "what you are" is an amorphous, oozy substance. Oozy substances have a variety of textures and dynamics. It could be a slippery, fish-innards substance; a poisonous, mercurial substance; or a sweet, sticky syrup. Those are three contrasting variations on ooze. Reading them conjures up strong images and reactions. We need to make clear choices: Understand why we're making them and how to express them.

Student Journal 5.2

All handout materials are available on the companion Web site at www.HumanKinetics.com/DanceComposition.

Exercise 5.3 Clowning

When Real Becomes Surreal

MUSIC SELECTION
Track 14

The exercise introduces over-the-top, a tool for comedic and dramatic physical theater.

Many North Americans equate clowns with children's parties and holiday parades. In the rest of the world, clowns are respected performers, and their art form receives serious attention. The art of clowning is an ancient one. It exists in numerous cultures, and though each culture provides a unique interpretation of the art, the concept of the clown is universal. Clowns embody our fears and sorrows, our pleasures, and our secret longings. Clowns can criticize when others can't. Whether it's a medieval court jester making fun of a king or 20th-century clowns of the Moscow circus during the Communist regime, clowns have liberties artists from other disciplines have not.

This exercise is based on the concept of going over the top—a basic clowning skill and of value to anyone studying physical theater. The premise is quite simple: Take a common action, such as waving to someone, tying a shoelace, or eating a sandwich, and play with the activity until the action (or object being manipulated) takes control. For example, a "hello" wave may become larger

"Bethany's Death" from the Gorgonetrevich Corps de Ballet National in Diana Kolpak's production of Bethany's Gate.
Diana Kolpak, photographer/director. dlkolpak@gmail.com.

and more frantic in the effort to get that certain someone's attention, then more dejected and forlorn for being ignored. Or a shoelace may grow longer and uncontrollable, and eventually it transforms into something predatory like a spider or snake.

There's a lot of repetition in over-the-top. Knowing how to manipulate movement is essential in dance. Playing with an action's size, weight, rhythm, texture, direction, and level is an important clowning skill, too.

Observation

Think of all the simple activities you perform every day: flossing teeth, brushing hair, sweeping the floor, cooking, eating, drying dishes, petting the dog. Select a mundane activity to work with during the Internal and External Exploration portions of the exercise.

Note to Facilitator

Read through the exploration before class and prepare your word list as described in steps 4 and 5.

Internal Exploration

1. Go to a spot away from others. Assume the approximate position or level needed for the selected activity (kneel to tie shoes, stand at the sink, sit to eat, and so on).
2. Breathe deeply and visualize the place where the activity is occurring and the objects you are using (dental floss, hairbrush, broom, or dog). Become physically engaged with the activity in as normal a way as it can be done without actually having the dental floss, hairbrush, broom, or dog at hand. See and feel the objects. Be committed to the task.
3. The activity, though repetitive, will evolve. Everything evolves (hair may get more tangled, the dog may become restless). Go with it: continue to floss, brush, and so on. After working in silence for 1 to 2 minutes, the music track in which a bell rings every 10 seconds will come on.
4. On the sound of the bell, the facilitator will call out a word and the objects must respond to them. That same word will be called out the entire length of the track so the object will keep becoming more of what is being called.
5. The music track is only 50 seconds long, but it will be repeated four to six times; and depending on the facilitator's decision, new words will be introduced. Actions and the objects must respond to the words. Words include *bigger, smaller, heavier, lighter, sticky, twisted,* and *crumpled*.
6. Objects may transform into something other than what it originally was. For example, the sweet, little dog might grow into a canine King Kong or a sandwich might disintegrate into crumbs. Don't let any surprises prevent you from working. Keep at it no matter what.

7. After the track has been played four times, there will be silence. Allow the object and actions to return to normal. To assist, the facilitator will count backward from 10 to 1, at which point all participants will stop and realign themselves with the original activity.

External Exploration

Divide into two groups and repeat the exercise while others watch. Audience members may call out instructions to those performing.

Group Reflection

- Go around the circle and contribute a personal over-the-top experience. (Almost squished a microscopic dog, almost drowned in dish water, and so on.)
- As a viewer, was it all madness, or was there some sense to the activity? (Were the words unifying—the audience sees everything getting smaller, stickier, weightless?)

Over-the-top takes real life to the extreme—beyond reality. Now sometimes (and not necessarily because we're lucky) we have an over-the-top experience during the normal course of a day. Those moments can be blissfully ecstatic walking-on-air days or they can be days where you feel like you're wearing a sign that says "kick me." Picture someone walking along the street when a car speeds by and drives through a huge puddle and sprays cold, smelly water all over him. A few minutes later, he buys a big, hot cup of coffee to take to work but bumps into someone and his coffee and the other person's coffee (of course) spills all over him. Then before he gets to work, a bird flies by overhead and . . . it's an over-the-top day.

Creation and Presentation

There are two variations: One uses mundane activity; the other uses technical elements of dance. Work in ensembles of four or five people. The first variation requires chairs.

Variation 1 (Using Everyday Movement)

As a class, come up with eight repetitive actions or activities people perform independently of each other and at their own time, but in the same room. (Make sure there is a different one for every ensemble.)

Those activities may include the following:

- Reading or researching at the library
- Eating at a restaurant
- Sewing clothes in a factory
- Working out in a weight room

Write each of the activities on separate pieces of paper. Fold each piece so the writing is hidden, then place the papers in a bag, hat, or shoebox.

Create another list of 10 to 12 descriptive movement words that aren't technical dance terms. Here are examples:

- Twist
- Crumble
- Float
- Quiver
- Pull
- Undulate

Write those words on separate pieces of paper and put them in a different container.

Place the chairs offstage at one side of the performance area. When an ensemble group is called, each of its members will pick their own descriptive word from the container and then go to the chairs and wait until an audience member pulls out one of the activities from the other container and calls it out. (Once an activity is used, it may not be used again, so don't return it to the bag, hat, or box.)

1. Upon hearing the activity or situation, ensemble members will, without discussion, take a chair, place it somewhere in the performance area, and begin to perform the task they believe best suits the situation.
2. After 10 to 15 seconds of normal activity, someone from the audience calls out, "Change!"
3. Then the activity and objects required for fulfilling the tasks will begin to shrink, float, or crumble as each person lets the action he's picked pull him out of reality and eventually into an extreme sense of over-the-top.
4. Each ensemble will work for approximately 2 minutes until someone from the audience signals a return to normal by slowly counting down from 10 to 1 (1 represents a normal level of activity).
5. After hearing "1," continue to work at normal for several breaths, then freeze.

After every ensemble has performed the exercise, sit together and discuss.

Group Reflection of Variation 1

- Was the over-the-top element magnified through people's performing the same activity but being affected very differently? If yes, describe how. (For example, one person's fast intensifies another person's slow.)
- How does this exercise build skills for character development?

Variation 2 (Using Dance Technique)

As a class, come up with at least eight relatively simple, repetitive actions from any dance technique. (Actions that might induce dizziness after numerous repetitions, such as spins and swings, are not appropriate.)

Write each of the activities on separate pieces of paper. Fold each piece so the writing is hidden, then place the papers in a bag, hat, or shoebox. Use the same list of descriptive words from the first variation.

As before, when an ensemble group is called to the performance area, each person will pick a descriptive word (such as crumble or float) so every member of an ensemble has her own over-the-top instruction. Then the ensemble will wait until the technical dance exercise they'll be working with is called out from the audience. (The dance exercises are now in the container the activities were in.)

- Upon hearing the activity or situation, ensemble members will, without discussion, place themselves in the performing area and begin to perform the task normally.
- After 10 to 15 seconds, someone from the audience will call, "Change!" and dancers will begin to let the action be manipulated by their descriptive word.
- The technical skill they are performing will shrink, float, or crumble. One person may crash wildly across the stage with arms flailing, while another may become twisted in a knot.
- Each ensemble will work for 2 minutes until the count down to "normal" is heard.
- Don't stop at 1; take several breaths of working at normal before finishing.

After every ensemble has performed the exercise, sit together and discuss.

Student Journal 5.3

All handout materials are available on the companion Web site at www.HumanKinetics.com/DanceComposition.

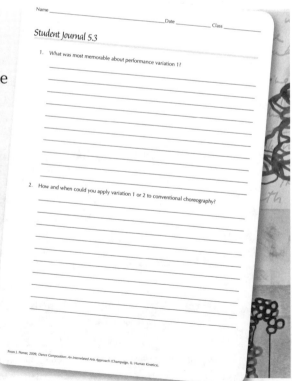

Final Group Reflection

This over-the-top variation explores what happens when extreme applications of weight, attack, and energy are imposed on technical dance exercises. What new insights did it bring to the technical skills being performed?

Arts Connection

Clowning has pathos. It expresses the human condition. Clowning explores the world in all its sadness and beauty and always through a sense of wonder. Silent-film stars Buster Keaton, Harold Lloyd, and Charlie Chaplin were masters of the art. In their movies, their characters didn't sugarcoat life; they presented the hardships of poverty, loneliness, and alienation in humorous, classic over-the-top fashion. One of my favorite film clowns is Jacques Tati's character Monsieur Hulot, who takes a critical view of modern life and technology. Choreographically speaking, Jacques Tati's films are absolutely brilliant. For more information on Jacques Tati's films, go to www.tativille.com or www.imagesjournal.com.

Artist Highlight Interview

"Wellspring," choreographed and performed by Denise Fujiwara.
Avril Patrick, photographer.
www.avrilpatrick.com.

Denise Fujiwara is one of Canada's most expressive contemporary dance artists; her performing career spans more than three decades. An award-winning choreographer, Denise performs internationally and delivers exploratory butoh-based movement workshops for movers of all backgrounds. Denise is the artistic director of Fujiwara Dance Inventions and the CanAsian International Dance Festival.

JP: **You've been performing and choreographing for over 30 years—the first 15 doing contemporary ensemble work, followed by 15 years as a solo dance artist with a strong butoh base. Now you're bringing your wealth of experience back to ensemble choreography. It's quite a journey.**

DF: In my 15 years as a contemporary dancer, I'd seen a number of butoh performances, but it was Natsu Nakajima's work that compelled me to learn more. Most of the butoh artists I'd seen before her were male, and there was something about Natsu's dance that struck a chord in me. Her work is emotionally moving, feminine, sophisticated, and life affirming. She's an artist of great ability and maturity.

A lot of contemporary dance is an expression of youth, athleticism, and relationship issues of interest to young people. The choreography is best danced by young people. At that time, I was becoming interested in what could be communicated beyond those themes, and here was Natsu showing me what was possible. The thematic content of her work is mature and deals with a whole life. The work was masterful: the choreography, design, costumes, and music. Her dance could create a whole world in the theater. I don't think anyone else could do what she was doing. And even she, I imagine, would not perform it the same way every time. Her work was so filled with inner life and subtext—it was inimitable and it's the inimitability of it that made it so compelling to me.

By the age of 39 I felt I had gone as far as I could with contemporary dance—as a dancer and a choreographer. I didn't know how to get to the next level on my own, and I had hope that I could get there through the insights that Natsu's work gave me. When I actually got the opportunity to work with Natsu, I decided if I couldn't learn how to get to that next step, I would quit dance. I felt there were enough mediocre choreographers in the world, and the world didn't need another one. So I set the stakes very high for myself. And the experience of working with Natsu was terribly difficult. Nothing I knew from all of my years of training seemed to be of any use to me. It was all wrong, all irrelevant. Butoh works on a different paradigm.

JP: **Every butoh artist I've seen interprets the form differently, but one of the commonalities is to strive to be wholly present in each movement. That presence creates a weight or intensity. So many other dance forms resist gravity; they strive to get higher, become lighter, to fly. Butoh embraces weight, density, and other earthy qualities.**

DF: Those are fundamental characteristics of butoh: presence, the weight, and the relationship to the earth.

JP: **Is that why so much of butoh is slow?**

DF: Well, to refer to the "time is a sandwich" theory you tell the children, it's because the sandwich is so full. If there was nothing in there, if you brought little of yourself to the movement, you could go fast, but time and space are given a kind of density. There's density to the intention of the movement. The dancer is processing a great deal of information in the moment and, well, that's as fast as one can go. And that's what I meant by the complexity of Natsu's choreography. Each movement was filled with compelling intensity.

JP: **Most soloists have an inner intensity.**

DF: When you work on solo choreography, you're learning about the art in its most austere situation because you can't rely on engaging your audience with rhythmic counterpoint between dancers or spatial relationships or emotional relationships between dancers. These are relatively easy to create, but as a soloist there's just you, this space, time, sound, and the audience. So how do you make something of that?

I'm very interested in character, so there is that development, although not necessarily in a literary or theatrical sense. The character may not have a name in the way one understands Ophelia to be a character. But I think in the creation of a dance solo, one looks into the great reservoir of what makes someone human, what humanity is, and chooses the very particular and universal elements that will make up the character for each solo. In a sense I don't choose the qualities; they intuitively arrive. Every dance is a great mystery. You never know what it's going to be until it arrives, and I think you have to do research and open yourself to the possibilities that the research suggests.

JP: **And by research, you're not talking about going to the library; your research is with your body: exploring movement, your responses, and breath.**

DF: I do go to the library in the early stages of the research, but yes, movement research is where you look for specific qualities and the movement vocabulary. In the early days I was focused on doing movement research and personal research. I would ask myself, *What are the issues that really provoke me at this moment, the issues that have my life in a stranglehold?* And I would use those issues as the foundation for a work. Solos are naturally personal and intimate. I think in the beginning of a career, you mine your own life for material, but then as you get older, as you do more work, you cast your nets farther and you look at other issues.

For example, I did the cycle of work on the natural elements. The elements are an excellent source because each element is so vast, contradictory, and evocative. The thing I was very worried about was doing clichés because the elements have been inspiration for artists through the ages. I tried to embody the elements as opposed to intellectualize them—to become earth, to become water. In the process I found I had very personal responses to the elements, and those responses became part of each of the pieces. In a sense I attempted to anthropomorphize the element, but I also found that each dance became a very personal statement.

JP: **You have a piece titled "Unearthed."**

DF: Yes, and you know some might think my work wouldn't be accessible to children and people who don't know anything about dance. But when I work outdoors, those people come upon it and are often enthralled. "Unearthed" is a very slow piece, and I'm dressed in a ragged dress that looks like an unraveling mummy, and I'm caked in mud. I look terrible and rather scary. When I was performing it outdoors in Newfoundland, the children who happened by the performance kept creeping forward, coming closer and closer to me. At the very end of the piece, I walked toward them, then turned away, and walked up a path. Well, the children followed me. They would have followed me to the end of the earth. And the presenter heard one of children, a little girl, say, "She's the most beautiful thing I've ever seen." There I was, caked in mud and all raggedy, and she saw the beauty in that. She saw the beauty beyond the superficial. It made all the work worthwhile to me in that moment.

"Unearthed," performed and choreographed by Denise Fujiwara.
Avril Patrick, photographer.
www.avrilpatrick.com.

JP: **I love to hear stories like that. It's one of the reasons site work is so important. You choreographed "Conference of the Birds," your first ensemble piece in 15 years, as an outdoor piece.**

DF: Yes. One of the reasons I wanted to do "Conference of the Birds" as a site piece is the fabulous experiences I've had doing dance in open spaces. It's refreshing to have new audiences, and it's wonderful for them to come upon contemporary dance, which for so many is an unexplored art form.

JP: **"Conference of the Birds" had a wonderful sense of breath. There was space—the clouds and sky. With Debbie Danbrook's shakuhachi and the whispered vocals, you created a piece full of lightness yet profoundly beautiful. Tell me a little about how you chose the piece and the choreographic process.**

DF: I came across it by accident. After 15 years of solo work, I decided to do a group piece and I was looking for some content. One night while I was driving home, I turned the radio on to the CBC radio program *Ideas*, and just when I turned it on they were talking about the poem "The Conference of the Birds." They read a bit of the original poem and I knew that that was the story for the dance.

The poem was written by the great Sufi philosopher Farid ud-Din Attar in the 12th century. It was a little intimidating at first. I thought, *Who am I to take a famous epic Sufi poem, a revered classic poem, and interpret it into contemporary dance?* I also knew about the Peter Brook version of "The Conference of the Birds." And I also thought, *Who am I to come after Peter Brook and do another version?* But it was the right vehicle. I decided to do an ensemble piece and I needed an ensemble journey. So I got a copy of the poem and read it, all the while wondering, *Can I immerse myself in this? Can I fully relate to this Sufi legend? Can I do it justice?* It's very complex and at the same time so open, and such a beautiful story that I think people of all backgrounds can relate to the work and believe in it fully.

JP: **In the poem as in your piece, the birds of the world have gathered together and must embark upon a long and dangerous journey. Each bird has its strengths as well as its weaknesses, and they face those weaknesses and discover inner strengths along the way. How did you decide who was to portray which bird?**

DF: I let the dancers choose which bird character they would be. Some knew immediately who they wanted to be. Some of them chose bird characters very much like themselves, and one dancer chose a bird character that was exactly the opposite of her and took that on as a challenge, which I thought was very brave of her. I gave each of the bird characters a score, and they created their own solos out of the score. Then we worked together to refine each solo and deepen it. So they all contributed to the development of the work.

JP: **Is that the process you use when you're commissioned to create a solo for someone else?**

DF: When I commission a choreographer to do a solo on me, I tend to choose choreographers who don't work like me so that they'll push me in a new direction, into the unknown, and challenge me. Each commission has pushed me as a performer.

Now I think the people who commission me appreciate the intimacy or the humanity of my solos. And in order to create those solos for myself, I've examined my most private ideas and feelings about things and put those into the dance. This creates a dilemma for me because when I work with other people, I don't feel I can prod them to the same degree. I can't ask them the same kinds of intimate questions I ask of myself.

JP: **I'm dying to know what types of questions you ask yourself.**

DF: Well, I guess you ask yourself, What are my foibles, the impediments in my life? What makes me sad? What am I most afraid of? What are my deepest desires? What makes me ecstatic? Why do I respond to things in this way, or that way? And in asking yourself hard questions and giving honest answers, you reveal something about your nature and reveal some aspect of real human behavior. I think that gives the piece a certain honesty. And when working with other people, I'm a little bit shy in asking them to be as honest and revealing as I can be with myself.

JP: **But it's part of the artistic process. Every artist asks herself questions, pushes herself, and sometimes puts a needle on her sore spot and jabs at it to find out why it makes her twitch.**

DF: Yes, but a choreographer has no right to demand that a dancer spill her guts.

JP: **No, of course not. That's why, when I'm teaching, I like to separate personal reflections from group discussions. We need to be honest with ourselves in the reflections, then choose what parts of our personal reflections we feel comfortable sharing in the group discussion. We need to keep some things to ourselves, but the insights we keep private get used; they become part of us and inform our dances.**

DF: Yes, like actors. They don't have to reveal to the director what they're using as subtext.

JP: **As long as the actor's getting the desired results.**

DF: Exactly. And using literary vehicles for ensemble choreography creates a buffer zone. When I was working on "Conference of the Birds," I could ask the dancers to interpret their movement work through the context of the poem. I didn't need to know what their subtext was. The poem gave them structure from which they could create.

JP: **And you're working on another literary-based ensemble piece?**

DF: I'm working on adapting Jean-Paul Sartre's play *No Exit*. When he wrote the play, Sartre asked what would happen if you locked three flawed strangers in a room for eternity. It's rife with complex relationships—spatial, temporal, interpersonal, and political.

For more information on Denise Fujiwara, go to www.fujiwaradance.com.

CHAPTER 6

Words, Thoughts, and Actions

Words are alive and languages grow. Whether we speak, write, or use sign language, words are evolving. An example is in the various forms of English used by writers over the centuries. Geoffrey Chaucer (1343-1400) wrote in the late Middle Ages. The English of Chaucer's time is vastly different from modern English. Chaucer's most famous work, *Tales of Canterbury* (in later centuries the title was changed to *The Canterbury Tales*), was written in what we now call Middle English. Here are the opening lines:

> Whan that April with his shoures sote
> The drought of Marche hath perced to the rote.

Put into modern English, it goes like this:

When April's sweet showers have pierced the drought of March to the root.

There are wide differences in spelling, pronunciation, and meaning between Middle and Modern English. By the time of William Shakespeare (1564-1616), the English language had evolved somewhat closer to the modern version, and Shakespeare himself was an influential factor in that growth. Over 2,000 words appear in his plays that had never before appeared in print. It's incredible to imagine one person having such an impact on language. Shakespeare is the most-produced playwright in the world. His works have been translated into almost every spoken language in the world (as well as sign language).

So how can we study the theatrical and literary arts without looking at words? Words are a writer's primary strength, just as muscles and bones are for a dancer. With words, writers carve images in the air. They compose with words; like a musician selecting one note over another, writers choose words not just for their meaning but also for their sonic and musical properties.

Words have resonance: the sound the word starts and ends with, the number of syllables, and the similarity or contrast of one word against another. Some words sound comforting; others sound harsh. Several languages have the sounds *o, a, p,* and *m* in their words for *mother* and *father*. Survey the class and try to complete the following list.

- English: ma, pa, mom, pop
- French: mama, papa
- Italian: _____
- Spanish: _____
- Hungarian: _____
- Hebrew: _____
- Arabic: _____
- Others: _____
- Dutch: _____
- German: _____
- Chinese: _____
- Japanese: _____
- Korean: _____
- Hindi: _____
- Russian: _____

There are several theories for why the sounds *m, o, a,* and *p* are so prevalent in words for *mother* and *father*. Some theories connect the *m, o,* and *a* sounds with the mouth movements infants make when calling out to be fed and while breast-feeding. Other theories explore language and human DNA coding. For those interested in studying linguistics, go to www.aber.ac.uk/media/Documents/S4B/sem01.html to read Professor Daniel Chandler's "Semiotics for Beginners." It's a great introduction to semiotics. The opening paragraph of the introduction section is smart and funny, and it supports many of the ideas regarding interconnectiveness presented in this text.

Before you begin to work on exercise 6.1, try this simple test:

1. Hold a tissue two to three inches (approximately 5-8 cm) away from your mouth.
2. Vocalize the *mmmm* sound. The tissue doesn't move, even though you can feel your mouth and lips buzzing with sonic energy.
3. Vocalize the *pppp* sound. As air shoots out from your mouth, it pushes the tissue outward. The letter *p* is sometimes referred to as an exploding consonant. The energy produced by making the *p* sound is vastly different from energy of the *m*.
4. Awareness of the sonic energy of a sound helps when you are translating it into movement. The *m* could be translated into inward motions, the *p* into outward motions.

But you don't need to know the science behind language or a word's etymology to participate in this exercise. Just let the words move you—let them speak to you sonically, emotionally, intellectually, and kinetically.

Exercise 6.1 Alliterations

MUSIC SELECTION
None

Exploring Sonic Properties of Consonants

This exercise develops awareness of the musicality of words and vocal confidence for those with limited voice experience.

Alliteration is a playful literary tool most commonly found in children's books and nursery rhymes, but it's also used selectively by playwrights and authors. Alliterations are sentences or phrases in which each word (or almost each word) starts with the same sound. "Fun-filled phonetic frolic" is an alliteration; so is "She sells seashells at the seashore." The advertising media employs alliterative devices as tools for coining catchy phrases. Alliterations are easy for consumers to remember.

Ana-Francisca de la Mora, Second Floor Collective, performing "Diálogo." Visual artist: Antonio Gómez-Palacio.
David Hou, photographer. www.davidhou.com.

Observation

Read this phrase aloud softly.

>Lithe, lazy lizards lounged languidly.

Did you feel the action of the tongue when pronouncing the *l* sound? Read it aloud again, and focus on the movements within the mouth. Feel the tongue touch the top of the upper teeth and gently shoot forward. Speak the phrase again and listen to the sonic qualities of the *l*; it could be described as breathy lightness.

Internal Exploration

Think of an action to communicate both the physical properties (tongue moving from upper teeth to front of mouth) and sonic properties (breathy lightness, or lilting quality) on the *l* sound. A small flicking action comes to mind.

1. Start by using a flick, and create a movement phrase that follows the alliterative phrase's sonic and rhythmic qualities. In order for the movement phrase to be an alliterative phrase, every movement must start with a flick. The sounds coming after the *l* are different for each word, so the movements should be different, too.
2. Try performing other light actions instead of a flick. Work those actions repetitively with the same part of the body, then rotate the action among the hand, arm, foot, leg, chin, and eyelid. Explore as wide a range of movement possibilities to interpret the *l* sound.
3. Don't work silently. Speak the phrase while moving.
4. Explore various movement relationships to the alliterative phrase for 3 to 5 minutes.

External Exploration

Choose one of the movements explored:

1. Present the alliterative phrase with two or three other people. Stand in the performance area. Before beginning, demonstrate the action selected to represent the *l* sound.
2. Vocalize the text while performing.
3. Repeat the phrase three times, then freeze until everyone in the group has finished.
4. Once everyone has presented, discuss the movement phrases.

Group Reflection

- Other than the suggested flicking, what movements were used to communicate the *l* sound?

- Did everyone speak the phrase with the same rhythm? If not, how did the rhythms differ, and what was the effect? (For example, exaggerating and lengthening the *l* meant that the action representing the *l* was much more elongated than a flick and perhaps contained some of the descriptive elements of the lllithe, lllazy, llllllanguid llllllizards.)
- Was it difficult to vocalize the text while performing? If yes, identify why. Was it because of breathlessness while moving or perhaps shyness?

Many of the exercises in this chapter require vocalizations, but this isn't something to fear. We walk and talk at the same time, and this is merely an extension.

Difficulty in moving while speaking and singing may be because of shallow breathing. If that's the case, develop a deeper sense of breath through this exercise:

1. Lie on the floor in neutral position.
2. Inhale. Starting with the diaphragm, slowly fill the torso with air, then just as slowly exhale. Feel how slow, deep inhalations and exhalations affect the mid-, upper, and lower torso. Try to always initiate the inhalation from the diaphragm. Work the inhalation and exhalation evenly. If the inhalation takes 5 beats, exhale for 5 beats. As control and awareness develop, the duration of each breath will too.
3. Use color to help visualize the breath: Inhale and fill your torso with golden light. Exhale and expel the golden light up into the air above you. As the exhalation becomes longer and steadier, you can imagine exhaling a line of light from your mouth to the ceiling. Continue breathing with this image for 30 to 60 seconds.
4. Add a sound to the color. It can be a simple sound to start. Inhale and fill the torso up like a balloon; exhale and expel the air with a soft *ssss* as the balloon deflates. Continue for 30 to 60 seconds.
5. Continue for another minute, exploring other consonant and vowel sounds.

Alliterations are musical, fun, nonsensical, and very easy to memorize. This exercise develops confidence while vocalizing, so take full advantage of the playful and childlike qualities. Imagine being back in elementary school. Listen to the sounds of children shouting on the playground or singing jump-rope songs.

Creation and Presentation

Before you begin, read these three new alliterative phrases:

- Green, greasy goo gushed from gray granite grates.
- Winifred wandered wistfully while wondering where William went.
- Ben broke Barry's bright blue bowl.

Each phrase features a different letter in the lead spot, and each letter has a distinct sonic quality. Take 2 to 3 minutes to vocalize all of the phrases in the following ways:

- Two times slowly and two times quickly
- Two times emphasizing the first letter of each word
- Two times while holding the palm of your hand approximately an inch (almost 3 cm) in front of your mouth

Work in pairs. Select one of the alliterative phrases to use as a foundation for a duet containing the following requirements:

- The alliterative phrase must be spoken aloud at least four times, and each time it should be vocalized differently. Both voices can speak the text together at the same time in the same way only once. There are numerous ways to vocalize text—think of it as an orchestration with rhythmic patterns, harmonies, and tempo and textural changes (apply skills explored in part 2 of this book).
- Perform the spoken text one time without any movement (it can be from off stage, in a frozen position on stage, and so on). This may be counted as one of the four vocal variations.
- Perform the duet without musical accompaniment—use only voices.
- Take 20 to 25 minutes to create and memorize the duet.

During creative work it's necessary for dancers to alternate between performing movements with full energy and marking things out. The same is true for voice work. Constant whispering won't expand the vocal range, so speak out and stretch the voice; work it high and low, clear and strong. Play the voice like an instrument: Use legato, staccato, and trills. The studio should be filled with the sound of voices. It can be distracting, but stay focused and stay connected visually and sonically.

When everyone is ready, present the duets one at a time. It's interesting to alternate the alliterative phrases. Have a duet working with *g* go first, followed by a duet working with *w*, followed by a duet working with *b*, and so on. Check beforehand to make sure there isn't one phrase that attracted a larger number of duets than the other two phrases. If that's the case, design a performance order with a balanced mix (*b, g, w, b, b, g, w, b, b,* and so on).

After all of the duets have performed, discuss the creative process and choreographic results.

Final Group Reflection

Each dancer should respond to the first two questions. Even if it's to express the same experience as others, it's important for everyone to contribute.

- What was the biggest challenge for you in this exercise (vocal shyness, singing off key, speaking and moving at the same time, and so on)? How did you overcome it?
- Compare strategies for overcoming these challenges. It's interesting to learn how many people faced the same challenge yet developed different strategies for overcoming them.
- Were there significant similarities or differences within the g, w, and b duets? If yes, identify. (For example, every duet used a canon sequence, or all of the b duets had a movement sequence featuring stamping or closed fists, and all the w duets had a windblown sensibility.)
- Were the dancers' faces more animated than usual?

Vocalizing while dancing moves the face. Connecting words to dance helps dancers develop subtext and emotional impulses to inform the movements, making each action more powerful and more dynamically charged. Exercise 3.1 worked on animating the face using rhythmic impulses; the exercises in this section follow a more theatrical approach.

Student Journal 6.1

All handout materials are available on the companion Web site at www.HumanKinetics.com/DanceComposition.

Arts Connections

Meredith Monk is a pioneer of experimental voice and dance theater. She has dozens of recordings, live performances, film, and video projects to her credit. Meredith Monk creates mesmerizing works of physical and sonic beauty incorporating movement, voice, music, lights, and drama. In 1968 she founded The House, a company dedicated to exploring interdisciplinary work; 10 years later she founded Meredith Monk and Ensemble. She is a prolific artist and teacher, and her voice has the emotional and spiritual richness of sounds sung from the heart, mind, and body. For more information on Meredith Monk, go to www.meredithmonk.org.

In classical East Indian dance forms (Bharatanatyam, Kathak, Kuchipudi, Manipuri, Mohiniyattam, and Odissi), facial expression is as important as hand and finger positions (mudras). The eyebrows rise and lower. The eyes dart from side to side, roll, expand, and contract. You could watch a close-up face shot of a Kathak or Mohiniyattam dancer and be absolutely riveted by the emotions and articulation of muscles that play across her face. For more information on classical East Indian dance, art, and music, go to www.culturalindia.net.

Exercise 6.2 Vowels and Syllabic Phrases

Sound, Action, and Emotional Connections

MUSIC SELECTION
Track 34

Observation

Warm ups that focus on exercising and animating facial muscles are neglected in most Western dance forms, but these skills are imperative for actors and singers.

Warm up the face.

1. Find a place to sit facing a wall or looking at someone's back several meters away. Avoid eye contact with others because it could be distracting.

2. Vigorously rub your face for 10 seconds. Then without using your hands to manipulate your face, perform these stretches:
   - Open the mouth as wide as possible. Hold for 10 to 20 seconds. (Keep breathing.)
   - Purse the lips and furrow the eyebrows to pinch the face as tightly as possible. Hold for 10 to 20 seconds. (Keep breathing.)
   - Puff the cheeks out as fully as possible. Hold for 10 to 20 seconds. (Keep breathing.)
   - "Chew" a large piece of gum on the right side of the mouth for 10 seconds, then on the left side of the mouth for 10 to 20 seconds. (Keep breathing.)
   - Stretch out the tongue and open the eyes as wide as possible (lion pose in hatha yoga). Hold for 10 to 20 seconds. (Keep breathing.)
   - Keep the head still while moving the eyes from side to side for 10 seconds.
   - Keep the head still while moving the eyes up and down for 10 seconds.
   - Rub your face for 10 seconds, then sit quietly with eyes closed for 20 seconds.

Internal Exploration

MUSIC SELECTION
Track 34

The sonic accompaniment features a voice exploring the letters *a*, *e*, *i*, *o*, and *u*. Try animating the face as you work with the music in the following ways:

- Isolate the face. Move the face by taking on the shape of the sounds being made.
- Work the full range of movement—face and body. Respond to the emotional energy and content of the sounds.

- Explore face and body movements that are connected to or disconnected from the sounds.
- Try not to be repetitive. Find various muscles to manipulate; explore different textures, tonal qualities, rhythms, emotions, and narratives. Improvise with the sonic stimuli and stay in the moment. Keep moving and keep breathing.

External Exploration

MUSIC SELECTION
Track 34

Half the class watches while the other half repeats the exercise. Those performing should arrange themselves so they're facing downstage. Performers may sit or stand in whatever position is most comfortable. The audience should try to be as discreet as possible. Avoid making eye contact or doing anything that might cause the performers to break their concentration and lose focus. After the first group has performed, switch roles so everyone has a chance to view the exercise.

Group Reflection

Everyone should contribute to the first and last question.

- How does your face feel now?
- While you were performing, did you discover facial muscles and movement capabilities you were previously unaware that you had? If yes, describe and demonstrate.
- Did you get emotionally involved while performing the exercise? If yes, can you articulate what happened or why that occurred?

Creation and Presentation

MUSIC SELECTION
Assigned vocalizations (in ensembles of four or five)

Exercise 6.1 (Alliterations) explored consonants. The first part of this exercise explored vowels. The next step is to combine consonants and vowels in syllabic phrases and create full-body movements to accompany them.

Work in groups of four or five to discover the sonic and movement potential of the following five phrases. Similar to the alliterative phrases, each syllabic phrase presents a unique combination of hard and soft sounds. Read each of the lines aloud three times, using the vocal qualities suggested:

1. (Whisper it) sawa-sata-ga, sawa-sata-go, sawa-sata-ga, sawa-sata-go (figure 6.1*a*).
2. (Enunciate it) veer-aki-aki baka veer-aki-ki, veer-aki-aki baka, veer-aki-ki (figure 6.1*b*).
3. (Undulate it) ooopa-ee-ooopaah, ooopa-ee-ay, ooopa-ee-ooopaah, ooopa-ee-ay.
4. (Slowly drone it) uzulufu, uzulufu, uzulufu.
5. (Bird-call it lightly) jet-tex jet-tex, jet-tex jet-tex.

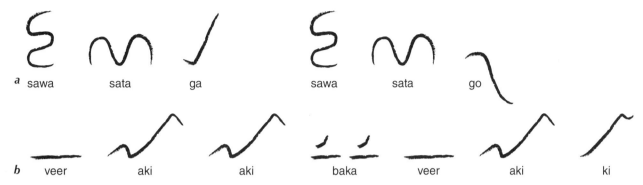

Figure 6.1 In phonetics, a soft *a* has an upside-down curve above it and a hard *a* has a straight line above it (not that different from music notation, is it?). Instead of writing the sounds out phonetically, it's interesting to translate them into abstract imagery, as seen in these illustrations of the wavy motion of (a) the *ahhh, ahhh* sound in *sawa* and (b) the sharper line translating *baka*. Whether we're writing real words or creating our own sonic notations, as figure 6.1 shows, we're using curves and angles—the same elements from exercise 1.1.

Repeat the phrases and explore movement possibilities for each phrase. Find other ways to vocalize the phrases (as opposed to whispering, droning, and so on) while moving.

Each phrase is a mixture of vowels and consonants with its own rhythm, sonic quality, character, and emotional energy. Use any three of the five syllabic phrases to create a sonic and movement work to the following story line:

- Use one syllabic phrase to establish a place or people (real or imaginary).
- Use one syllabic phrase to communicate a significant change to that place (natural disaster, war, day to night, discovery of an object, birth, union, and so on).
- Use a third syllabic phrase to illustrate how the change has affected the place or people.
- Movement must accompany the syllabic phrases. There may be times when the movement and sound are performed separately, but for the most part they should be performed simultaneously.
- This exercise can be approached as a short study or an in-depth choreographic project requiring lengthy creation and rehearsal time. Facilitators should make expectations clear to ensembles.

Final Group Reflection

After the presentation, representatives from each ensemble should answer the questions:

- Explain how your group developed its story line and clarify the ideas behind each section.
- Did your ensemble consciously use musical skills introduced and developed in the exercises from chapters 3 and 4? If yes, which ones?

Student Journal 6.2

All handout materials are available on the companion Web site at www.HumanKinetics.com/DanceComposition.

Arts Connections

Having a sonic or movement chorus tell the story of Little Red Riding Hood as suggested in the student journal is similar to the use of the chorus in classical Greek theater. The structure is as pertinent today as it was over 2,500 years ago. Tragedies such as Electra and Oedipus have been translated countless times over the centuries and have been adapted for opera, ballet, and film. They were a source of inspiration for many of Martha Graham's choreographic masterpieces, and Tadashi Suzuki, one of Japan's most acclaimed avant-garde theater directors, created a body of work that focuses on classical Greek drama. As a theatrical tool, the Greek chorus has inspired countless playwrights. T.S. Eliot's play *Murder in the Cathedral* has a chorus of cloistered nuns in the role of the chorus. They call out forewarnings of doom to the soon-to-be-murdered Archbishop of Canterbury.

Notation in 20th-century music and dance has much in common with visual arts. Concrete poetry also connects with visual art. Just as music can sound the way a person feels (such as gloomy or joyous), in concrete poetry the poems can look like what they are about, or the image can contrast the text to create tension. Concrete poetry became popular in the mid-20th century but by no means originated then. There are examples of concrete poetry from ancient Greece. There remain examples of words carved into stone not as they would normally have been written but artistically rendered to create an image. One could argue that there is an element of concrete poetry in all pictographic or calligraphic languages. And then there's graffiti.

For information on concrete poetry and other poetic forms, go to www.ubu.com.

Exercise 6.3 Soliloquy

Creating a Solo From the Inside Out

MUSIC SELECTION
Work in silence until creation, then use any atmospheric piece

A soliloquy is a speech made by an actor when he is alone on stage. A playwright uses this device to give the audience greater understanding of the character's depth and complexity. These speeches often express profound emotion or convey internal struggles, shifting attitudes, and changes of heart.

Soliloquies have been described as thought projection, and that same term can be used in describing a dance solo. Through movement, not text, dancers project their thoughts, emotions, and internal images. This exercise deepens the connection between external actions and internal thoughts. Instead of voicing thoughts aloud, a dancer creates the tension of a spoken soliloquy through movement and consciously projects the character's inner struggle to the audience. To do this, a dancer needs to develop internal images and voices. Without thought behind an action, what is there to project?

Observation

Even those who've never studied Shakespeare are acquainted with the titles of many of his plays and can quote a phrase or two of text. Lines from Shakespeare's plays have become part of our lexicon. *To be or not to be* are the opening words of one of Shakespeare's most well-known soliloquies. It's found in act 3, scene

Storyteller, dancer, and musician Emerita Emerencia performing in a dance Immersion Showcase Presentation.

David Hou, photographer. www.davidhou.com.

1 of *Hamlet, Prince of Denmark*. Throughout the play, Hamlet is plagued with doubt and indecision about himself, his family, and his friends. Many of his internal struggles are conveyed in soliloquies. When Hamlet ponders "To be or not to be," he's deliberating, weighing his options, looking for release from his troubles and wondering not just about ending his life but about what life, if any, exists afterward.

The first 12 lines of the soliloquy go as follows:

> To be or not to be, that is the question;
> Whether 'tis nobler in the mind to suffer
> The slings and arrows of outrageous fortune,
> Or to take arms against a sea of troubles,
> And by opposing, end them. To die: to sleep,
> No more, and by a sleep to say we end
> The heart-ache, and the thousand natural shocks
> That flesh is heir to: 'tis a consummation
> Devoutly to be wished. To die, to sleep;
> To sleep perchance to dream: ay, there's the rub
> For in that sleep of death what dreams may come,
> When we have shuffled off this mortal coil,

Internal Exploration

MUSIC SELECTION
Silence

Part 1

Dancers need to perform the exercise while moving in a straight line. To avoid collisions, designate the working spaces before beginning.

1. Stand in a straight line against one wall, looking out toward the wall at the opposite end of the room (at least 20 feet, or about 6 meters, away) two or three body lengths apart to create individual aisles. Dancers have complete freedom of movement within their aisles. During the exploration, everyone needs ease of access while they move back and forth between the walls. Try not to interfere with others by crossing over into their space.

2. In the first exploration, the far wall represents something (person, place, time, state of being) you want or dream about. Move toward it with desire, excitement, or perhaps shyness; move away from it with reluctance, sorrow, or regret.

3. The exploration will last at least 5 minutes.

4. Stay with the same image for several approaches, but each journey toward and away should be different. Try not to repeat yourself. That "something" should change throughout the exercise; don't get stuck on one image or idea for the entire time. Move quickly or slowly, directly or indirectly. Keep the images and ideas of desire clear in your mind.

5. This is a physical and emotional journey. Your feelings about moving toward and moving away from that image are important. There are numerous emotions to explore: doubt, fear, excitement, anxiety, longing, and contentment. Stay in touch with those feelings and stay focused on the journey.

Part 2

1. Now explore ways of moving toward and away from an undesirable person, event, or place. Once again, that "something" should change throughout the exercise. Try not to get stuck on one image or idea.

2. How does it feel going toward something you dread? It can be slow and painful, filled with trepidation. Sometimes, things require expediency, such as pulling off a bandage—just plunge in. And afterward, how does it feel? Is there relief, exhaustion, calm? Explore different approaches and work with a variety of images and ideas.

External Exploration

Divide into two groups and repeat both parts of the exploration (half of the class performs while the others watch).

Group Reflection

- What were the significant differences between part 1 and part 2 of the exercise?

- Survey the class on the types of images and ideas visualized in the first variation of the exercise and types of images and ideas used for the second. Discuss the similarities and differences.

- This exercise demands personal comment and intensity. How does that emotional intensity translate for the viewer?

Creation and Presentation

MUSIC SELECTION
Any atmospheric track

Use experiences from the explorations as a foundation for solo choreography based on a personal dilemma. Explore contrasting or conflicting emotions and ideas. Allow them to meet, struggle, and ultimately find a way to coexist.

Solos should contain these elements:

- Direction: a sense of moving toward and away
- Indecision: shapes pulling apart or pushing inward
- Hesitation: stuttering or stumbling
- Rest: a held balance or imbalance

Employ all the knowledge gained from the visualization work and explore a range of emotions and facial expressions.

This solo can be a short piece created in 20 minutes with a structure and improvised elements, or it can be a much longer, precisely choreographed work. Both approaches produce choreography with equally successful results. The facilitator will establish the following:

- How long the solo should be
- How much time there is to work on the piece
- When the presentation must be ready
- Presentation order

If the work is being completed in 20 minutes and all the pieces must be seen in one class, the solos can be performed two at a time. For longer, more crafted solos, present one by one, with no more than a third of the class presenting each day. When all of the solos for the day have been presented, discuss the work.

Final Group Reflection

Each performer should answer the first question.

- What two main images or ideas were you projecting outward?
- Were those images conveyed to the viewing audience? If not, what images or ideas did you feel or see?
- Was one of the four required choreographic elements more compelling than the others? If yes, why? (For example, one had the greatest potential for variation.)

Student Journal 6.3

All handout materials are available on the companion Web site at www.HumanKinetics.com/DanceComposition.

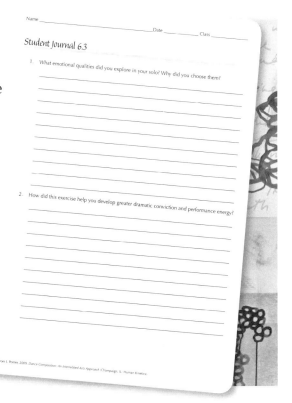

Exercise 6.4 Monologue

MUSIC SELECTION
None

Combining Text and Movement

The challenge is to create simple yet emotion-filled text that can be joined with movement.

Observation

The only type of word that can be placed between two pronouns to form a complete sentence is a verb. Verbs are action words that move us physically, such as *kick* and *push*, and emotionally, such as *envy* and *loathe*. The word *am* is also a verb. It's the first-person singular of the verb *be*. (Does being reminded that *be* is a verb make Hamlet's question of "To be or not to be" more potent?) *Am* is in the present tense and *was* is in the past tense. Either tense may be used to complete this type of sentence.

For example, the sentence *I envy you* is in the present tense and *I envied you* is in the past tense. Both sentences require only the one word to make it whole. The future tense doesn't work for this exercise because you would have to add an additional word to make it grammatically correct. *You will envy me* is inadmissible.

But the limit of one word per sentence needn't make the sentences boring or repetitive. There are many ways to make these short sentences expressive—try altering the punctuation. *I envy you* conveys admiration, whereas *I envied you?* can convey anger, dismay, or ridicule.

Internal Exploration

The following incomplete sentences are also on the student handout. Take 2 to 3 minutes to first write a list of 20 verbs, then select 8 of them to create 8 different sentences. No verb may be used more than once. Obvious verbs such as *kicked* or *pushed* may be used to complete one or two sentences, but other verbs such as *trust* or *ignore* have greater emotional and narrative content.

I _____ you.	I _____ you.
I _____ you.	I _____ you.
You _____ me.	You _____ me.
You _____ me.	You _____ me.

External Exploration

Get into two or three groups. Each group will form its own circle with all members of the group facing inward and standing in neutral position. One person in each circle will start by turning to the person to the right and saying, "I [insert one word] you." While speaking, incorporate movement. The movement may be literal or abstract—whatever first springs to mind. Immediately after, the person to whom the phrase was directed will turn and speak a new phrase to the next person. Use new verbs and different tenses and punctuation. A phrase may be screamed, whispered, whined, or hissed. Let the vocal expressions inform the accompanying movement. Words and actions can jump, twist, glower, and shake.

Go around the circle as many times as possible without repeating a phrase. Work for 3 to 5 minutes. Start the exercise again using "You [insert a word] me." Once again, work for 3 to 5 minutes to find as many words as possible to complete the phrase.

Group Reflection

Share some of the more unusual words discovered in this exploration.

- Do a show-of-hands survey of the class to find out who compiled a list of 20 or more verbs in the internal observation. After working in the circle, how many people feel they could add to their list of words? (If several students were unable to complete the list of 20 verbs and now think they can, give them a minute to do so.)
- When working in the group, did you find yourself repeating words others had said? If yes, how did you make the phrase different? (Change emotion vocally, physically, and so on.)
- When performing actions with the sentences, was it easiest to be literal, abstract, or a combination of both?

Creation and Presentation

This exercise may be an out-of-class assignment. Expectations regarding length of time of piece, creation and rehearsal time, and performance schedule should be determined at the outset.

1. The explorations may have introduced new vocabulary that you might wish to employ. Create eight new sentences and use those sentences as the foundation for a solo movement piece with voice. To make things more interesting, you may wish to use a variety of pronouns.

   I/you/he/she/they _____ me/you/him/her/them/it.

   Here are examples: *He rejected me. She ignored me. I trusted them.*

2. Select words based on their emotional and physical motivational strength. All eight lines must be spoken at some time in this solo. Try manipulating them in the following ways:
   - Change the order of the lines.
   - Repeat any of the lines any number of times.
   - Have sections containing movement without voice.
   - Have sections containing voice without movement.
   - Have sections containing movement and voice at the same time.

3. While working on the solo, be clear about what is being said and to whom it's being spoken. Is it a person from the past or present, or is it someone imagined in the future?
4. Use the skills developed throughout this section: vocal expression, emotional range, and commitment to character.

Final Group Reflection

- How did choreographing and performing this structure compare with working on the soliloquy from the previous exercise?
- Did the text and movement always have to make literal sense in order for it to work? If not, identify the most successful moments of nonliteral movements and text combinations and discuss why the voice and movement connection worked so well.

Student Journal 6.4a

All handout materials are available on the companion Web site at www.HumanKinetics.com/DanceComposition.

Student Journal 6.4b

All handout materials are available on the companion Web site at www.HumanKinetics.com/DanceComposition.

Arts Connection

The latter part of the 20th century gave birth to many popular one-man plays. British playwright, novelist, and musician Willy Russell created a theatrical tour de force for often-ignored actresses in their 40s. His work *Shirley Valentine* premiered in 1986 in Liverpool. It was produced in London in 1988, where it was so successful that it was immediately adapted for film in 1989 starring Pauline Collins, the actress who played Shirley in the London production. She's brilliant. The writing is hilarious, poignant, human, and honest. The entire play is a monologue. (The film adaptation includes some of the original monologues.) Russell has Shirley speaking to the audience and inanimate objects, with whom she's quite friendly. In act 1, scene 1, Shirley talks to the kitchen wall while preparing dinner for her husband. It's clear from the outset that she has a closer relationship to "Wall" than with any other member of her family. In act 2, scene 1, Shirley's in Greece talking to "Rock," her newfound friend. Rock is a rock on the beach. For more information about Willy Russell and his other plays (including *Educating Rita*), go to www.willyrussell.com.

Exercise 6.5 Dialogue

MUSIC SELECTION
None

Text and Subtext in Movement Duets

This is an extension of exercise 6.4. The text from the solos is reworked into dialogue.

Do we always say what we mean and mean what we say? Certainly not. Whenever there's text, there's the potential for inner meaning. Think of it in terms of an equation. Sometimes the upper half (text) and lower half (subtext) of an equation are equal: 2/2. You call out, "Help!" and you need it, but there are times when what is said and what is meant are not united. And of course, you may mean what you say, but it's interpreted differently than intended. Words are tricky. Their meaning changes over the centuries and from culture to culture.

Observation

Conversations have shapes (circular or pointed), rhythms (repetitive or random), and other dynamic elements used in dance.

Everyone's had conversations that repeat or go nowhere. There are several reasons for that: daily routines and habits and unresolved struggles, or sometimes it's because each person is so caught up in her own thoughts that she never really listens to what the other person is saying.

Internal Exploration

Work with a partner. Sit and explore the dramatic potential of the text using lines from the previous exercise to create a conversation. There is no movement in

Lin Snelling (foreground) and Hetty King perform movement and text in "Words."
Michael Reinhart, photographer.
www.quebec-elan.org/showcase/display/portfolio/71.

this exploration. Don't write things out; improvise with the text. Use the lines in any order, leave some out, play with the words, repeat your own or your partner's lines as often as you like. Here are two examples:

A: I used you.

B: **I** used **you.**

A: You used me?

B: I used you.

C: She ignored me.

D: Ignored.

C: He rejected me.

D: Rejected.

C: Ignored. Rejected.

D: I envy you.

Remember, conversations don't always make sense, so don't worry if there are disconnected phrases. Try to find a place, time, character, or emotion where the subtext can connect. Work for 3 minutes and keep exploring possible variations. Often the most interesting ones aren't the most obvious.

External Exploration

Each duet will perform a 1-minute improvisation of their dialogue for the class. The facilitator will watch the clock and announce, "Start" and "Finish" when the time is up. This is a vocal exploration without movement. Work vocal repetitions, pauses, tempo changes (one person speaks many lines quickly while the other responds slowly with one line), pitch, volume, and so on.

Discuss the exercise after everyone has presented.

Group Reflection

- Were people able to manipulate the text and subtext as easily as they manipulate movement? If not, why? What were the biggest challenges?
- Identify some of the most successful dialogues and discuss the reasons for their success. Was it the chance meeting of lines, the vocal or emotional range of the performance, understanding of subtext, or commitment to character?

Creation and Presentation

Work with the same partner and choreograph a duet containing no more than 6 of the 16 lines available. Find commonalities and contrasts. Work with the text and the subtext using these required elements to create a 2- to 3-minute piece:

- Use all or segmented parts of the chosen sentences. (By taking select words and using repetition, some of the text could be *Loathe, loathe, loathe, loathe. He. She. Me.*)

- Dance or move throughout the stage area in silence or while speaking.
- Find moments of stillness or silence.
- Most important, remember that even though the text is limited, the subtext may change throughout the piece.

This choreographic assignment will need physical and sonic space and requires preparation outside of class. The facilitator will establish time limits and a performance schedule. After all the duets have presented, discuss the work.

Final Group Reflection

- Each duet had a limited number of lines to work with, but did that prevent the characters and dramatic or dynamic intensity from developing? If yes, why? If no, what happened?
- Was vocal strength or confidence an issue? How many duets warmed up their voices before each rehearsal? How did this affect vocal range and skill?

Student Journal 6.5

All handout materials are available on the companion Web site at www.HumanKinetics.com/DanceComposition.

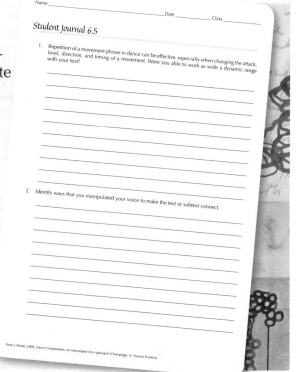

Arts Connection

Samuel Beckett's *Waiting for Godot* is one of the great theatrical works of the 20th century. As in Shakespeare's *Hamlet*, elements of doubt and disillusionment are explored. Described by Beckett as a "tragicomedy," the verbal and physical interplay between the two main characters, Vladimir and Estragon, creates a profound statement of the human condition. The lines are short and often repetitive. The play is in two acts. At the end of act 1, Estragon says to Vladimir, "Well, shall we go?" The other responds, "Yes, let's go," yet neither one moves. This is repeated at the end of act 2 when Vladimir says to Estragon, "Well, shall we go?" and Estragon replies, "Yes, let's go." Once again, neither moves. There are numerous books on Samuel Beckett, his life, and his writing. The Web site www.samuel-beckett.net is an introduction to this master playwright.

Culminating Exercise for Dance and the Dramatic and Literary Arts

The culminating exercise will be used for assessment purposes. The facilitator may use the rubrics, the student self-evaluation form, or both.

Storytelling

Create a Dance Based on a Traditional Folktale

"Cap o' Rushes" and "Sugar and Salt" are two well-known titles of the European folktale about a powerful king and his three daughters. The tale in its many versions existed long before Shakespeare wrote *King Lear* (his play about a king and his three daughters). Shakespeare's work is far more evolved and complex, but this wise and simple folktale was the nucleus of his play.

Observation

Traditional folktales have been the foundation for great works of literature and drama for centuries. They have also inspired some of the world's greatest ballets. Staying true to that tradition, a simple tale will be used as the foundation for the culminating exercise in this section.

The following is my adaptation of one of Aesop's fables, "The North Wind and the Sun." This tale is adaptable for a dance piece; it has wonderful tension between characters and it offers a wide range of movement.

The North Wind and the Sun

The North Wind and the Sun were talking one day. Their conversation turned into an argument with each claiming he was more powerful than the other.
"We need a test to prove which of us is stronger," said the North Wind.
"Agreed," said the Sun, and he turned his gaze upon the earth. "Do you see that man walking below us?" asked the Sun.
"My vision's fine," replied the North Wind. "Of course I do."
"I propose we settle the matter by seeing which of us can get his coat off faster. Whoever succeeds is the victor."

The North Wind couldn't be happier. "You designed the test, so I shall be the first to try." And with that, the North Wind blasted cold air on the man and viciously whirled and swirled around him. The North Wind's attack was so strong that the man's coat almost flew off his back. Laughing, the North Wind blew down even harder, but the man was fearful of losing his coat in the sudden wintry storm, so he held on tight. Even though the North Wind raged with all his might, he couldn't separate the man from his coat.

Eventually the North Wind admitted defeat and let the Sun take his turn. The Sun looked down at the windblown figure and beamed rays of warmth upon the man's back. The North Wind frowned while the Sun smiled gently and glowed a deep golden hue. The man, who had been shivering, relaxed and looked up at the now-clear blue sky. As he walked on, the air grew hot and beads of sweat appeared on his forehead. The Sun looked pleased and continued to beam down his warm, penetrating rays. Soon the man took off his coat and the North Wind begrudgingly declared the Sun the victor.

The student handout contains the fable and space for notes. Take 10 to 15 minutes to do the following:

1. Read the story two or three times.
2. Make notes of ideas these first readings conjured up (movement, text, props, costumes).
3. Fables contain morals. Sum up the moral in your own words and briefly articulate how it applies to personal relationships or world-reaching current events.

Creation and Presentation

Form a trio (the facilitator will make sure the trios are composed of dancers who haven't worked together recently). Together, adapt the story into dance. Share notes to see if there are similar interpretations and ideas about the story. Use those notes in establishing a starting point. Before beginning to develop additional ideas, look at the list of requirements to see what other elements you need to consider.

Required Elements

The adaptation of "The North Wind and the Sun" should contain the following elements:

- Short solos to establish each of the characters
- Duets between these characters:
    - The Sun and the North Wind
    - The North Wind and the man
    - The Sun and the man
- Create your own score using at least two of the following:
    - Rhythmic hand clapping, stomping, and other body sounds
    - Found sounds (is it possible to integrate found sounds with costumes or props?)
    - Recordings of music

- Spoken or chanted syllabic phrases
- Computer-assisted sound design using the Audacity program
- An artistic statement about the piece and the process (include a short biography of Aesop)
- Additional work should include the following:
  - Use of text in the performance
  - Costumes, masks, sets, and props
  - Possible alternative lighting

This project draws on skills developed while working throughout the book. It's a large project, so the work should be divided among the trio. For example, one person masters the soundscape (all contribute, but final editing creates the "master"), another draws up the lighting plots or coordinates the costumes, and the third crafts the artistic statement (after everyone has contributed ideas). Be organized, be responsible, and communicate with each other. If any problems arise, let your facilitator know immediately.

Your facilitator will establish a schedule clearly stating the following:

- How long you have to create and rehearse
- Minimum and maximum length of time for the piece
- A presentation schedule (no more than four per class period)

Have the artistic statement photocopied for audience members in time for the performance.

Final Group Reflection

Sitting through the presentations shouldn't feel repetitive. It's fascinating to see how differently a story can be told and equally fascinating to read about an ensemble's creative journey.

- Identify the most effective interpretations of the required elements and discuss why they were so successful.
- Did ensembles tell the fable from different perspectives (such as from the man's point of view, as the fable relates to current world issues, and so on)? If so, was one more unique or insightful or entertaining than the others?
- Were there any outstanding elements in any of the artistic statements (detailed biography of Aesop, intriguing overview of the dance, and so on)?

This is the final exercise in the book, but it's by no means the end. The exercises, Arts Connections, and Artist Highlight Interviews should inspire you to continue working in a multidisciplinary fashion, exploring traditional and experimental combinations of dance, visual art, music, and the dramatic and literary arts. As the image of the spiral path leading up the mountain suggests, endings are beginnings. Years ago at the end of a course I taught in Regina,

Saskatchewan, one of my students presented me with a brush painting he had made. Underneath it he wrote, "Only when the flower stops opening does it begin to fade. Thank you for opening my eyes." I was honored to receive the gift and often remind myself of his words. Inspiration is everywhere. Stay engaged: eyes seeing, ears listening, words forming, bodies pulsing.

Student Journal for Culminating Exercise for Dance and the Dramatic and Literary Arts

All handout materials are available on the companion Web site at www.HumanKinetics.com/DanceComposition.

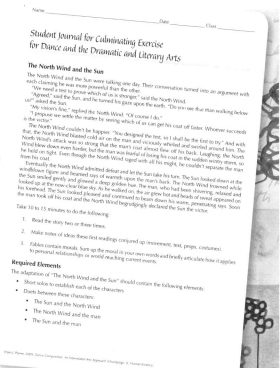

Self-Evaluation for Dance and the Dramatic and Literary Arts

All handout materials are available on the companion Web site at www.HumanKinetics.com/DanceComposition.

Rubric for Culminating Exercise for Dance and the Dramatic and Literary Arts

All handout materials are available on the companion Web site at www.HumanKinetics.com/DanceComposition.

Artist Highlight Interview

Emerita Emerencia performing in a dance Immersion Showcase Presentation.
David Hou, photographer.
www.davidhou.com.

Emerita Emerencia is an Aruban-born, award-winning multi-disciplinary artist. Emerita Emerencia has been touring solo since 1990, bringing her own style of performance (a fusion of theater, storytelling, percussive music, and dance) to audiences in Canada, the United States, Africa, and the Caribbean. Emerita taught dance at the University of Toronto for over 15 years, has been a guest artist at the dance department and the faculty of education at York University, and worked with postgraduate education students at the Ontario Institute for Studies in Education. The list of outstanding performing companies she has worked with include Soulpepper Theatre, b current Theatre, Tafelmusik Baroque Orchestra, the National Ballet of Canada, the Canadian Opera Company, and dance Immersion.

JP: **When I first saw your work, you were an actor and choreographer. Later I came to know you as a storyteller and musician. You're comfortable performing in so many disciplines. How do you choose what to do and when to do it?**

EE: People ask me, "Are you an actor? Are you a dancer? Are you a singer?" I say "All of the above." That's what I do. I integrate all of the art forms to serve the projects I work on. If I don't have the words to describe something, I'll use a movement, or if movement doesn't work I'll use a particular sound or song. If there needs to be something tangible, something the audience can see, I'll create it. And sometimes the medicine is in the story. You just have to tell the story in order for the message to really hit people, and a powerful story will tell you where the music should go and when the movement should come in. I move the audience with my body, with facial expressions, with music, and with audience participation, which to me is an art form in its own right. Not every performer knows how to do it; it's not easy. You have to read so many elements on the spot and be able to respond quickly. You need to be spontaneous and have great improvisational skills.

JP: **How did you develop skills in all of these areas?**

EE: I started off as an educator; that's what I trained for in Aruba. When I came to Canada, that went out the window. I couldn't teach in a public school.

JP: **Why?**

EE: I didn't have a BA from a Canadian University or an Ontario Teacher's Certificate, so I ended up teaching in a private school where those things weren't so important. While I was there, opportunity came knocking. I had the chance to audition for Black Theatre Canada. I'd never had an audition before and had no idea that I had to prepare for it. I just went there and they said, "What are you dancing for us today?" and I said, "I didn't know I'm supposed to prepare something." So they said, "Can you dance?" and I said, "Sure, sure I can dance." And they put on Stevie Wonder—this is a while ago, right—and I danced all my best club and disco moves. And they laughed. "Okay, read this piece of poetry." Well, they might as well have given it to me upside down; I couldn't make sense of it. Then they wanted a song, and I didn't even know any English songs, so I sang them a lullaby in Papiamento. They laughed at that, too. I left feeling terrible, but the next day I received a call telling me I got the part! Can you believe it? They hired me with no experience. Everyone else was experienced and well trained, and then there was me.

JP: **You'd never performed before and had no training, but they obviously recognized your potential. Did you do anything in your childhood to prepare you for a life in the performing arts?**

EE: I've thought about this, and the only thing I've come up with is that I'm Aruban and people from Aruba, or that part of the world—Dutch Caribbean—speak many languages. I speak five fluently, which means I'm connected to all these different cultures. I was raised in a community where there were at the least 15 nationalities and we all learned from each other. It was a thing of pride. We had the gift of language and we had the gift of culture and all the sensibilities that go along with it.

It's not just about the language; it's about every sensibility. I speak Spanish, and I dance the mambo. I understand where it comes from, and I know the people who dance it. I know how Cubans speak Spanish differently from the Mexicans, and the Spanish there is different from Spanish in Venezuela, the Dominican Republic, and other countries. Then add to the mix English, French, and Dutch influences and you can understand how growing up with these riches gives you an amazing ability to be flexible, to be adaptable, to be a shape shifter.

JP: **"Shape shifting" is a beautiful description of what performing artists do.**

EE: Yes, and that was my upbringing, my community, and my home. My father always made sure he taught us everything he knew about dance. He taught me the tango, the tumba, the cumbia, the guanguanco, the merengue—not just the steps, but the history to go with it. He would say, "You know, in your grandfather's days, this song came about . . ." and he'd give you the whole story. And look, I'm hearing a story—with its social, political, historical commentary—and learning a dance and singing the music all together. I've been doing this my whole life.

JP: **You can't separate the dance from the story or the story from the dance.**

EE: No, and in Aruba we also have knowledge of Jamaican, Haitian, and Trinidadian music and culture. Music is a great form of storytelling because behind every piece of music there's a story, and the stories come from everywhere. They came all the way from Africa and mixed with people from all over the world, including the people who first lived there, the aboriginals, even though a lot of that way of life was lost. And when I came to Canada, I was very interested in learning about aboriginal culture, and I am always open to new ways of seeing things.

JP: **You were working professionally without formal training, but did you have any significant mentors along the way?**

EE: In the early 1980s I received a Chalmers study grant, which allowed me to apprentice with Broadway producer Woody King Jr. in New York. At the time, Woody King Jr. was best known for producing *For Colored Girls Who Have Considered Suicide* by Ntozake Shange. He produced incredible work. I was there for six months, and in that time I did everything. During the day I was an assistant director. He produced a season and had several directors engaged, so I'd do whatever needed to be done: take notes, get props, sweep the floor, learn the lights, everything. When the shows went on tour, I did sound, set the props, looked after costumes, stage-managed. At night when we weren't on the road and there wasn't a show, I studied acting. I worked on two productions, one African American, one Chinese American. The Chinese American production was called *Dance and the Railroad* by David Henry Hwang. That show did very well and moved to Joe Papp's Public Theater in New York City. It played there for six months during the 1980-81 season and won three Obie Awards, which led to the cable television production of the same title, *Dance and the Railroad*. It was directed by and costarred John Lone. The work was exhausting but inspiring, and Woody King Jr. was incredibly supportive.

JP: **What happened when you returned to Toronto?**

EE: Well, I started working again with Black Theatre Canada. The first thing I did with them was play the role of Hermia in their Caribbean version of Shakespeare's *A Midsummer Night's Dream*. They also asked me to be the cochoreographer, so I'm acting, and Hermia's a big role, and on top of that I'm dealing with music and dance. And because the design of costumes would affect the movements, I was working with costume design, too.

We won a Dora Award for Artistic Excellence and Innovation for that production. It was so innovative and we had no money, and on top of that Canadian Stage had its own production of *A Midsummer Night's Dream*. They had a huge budget and we had a fraction of funding in comparison, but we were creative, and they recognized that.

Emerita Emerencia performing in a dance Immersion Showcase Presentation.
David Hou, photographer. www.davidhou.com.

JP: **That was an exciting time for you.**

EE: It was. I get back from New York, I'm doing Shakespeare, we win a big award, I get some television and film work, and things are going well for a while, but then I got stuck. Casting people just didn't know what to do with me and I didn't want to be doing little stereotyped roles forever—I was too politically aware and didn't want to fall into that. So I started doing a lot of theater and storytelling on my own in the schools. And people started hearing about me.

The Royal Ontario Museum asked if I could do a show dealing with African animals for one of their exhibitions. While I was working on that, I received a call from my father telling me that my grandmother was dying. She was 99. When I left Aruba, she made me promise her two things: that I would keep her memory alive and that, no matter where I was living, I would come back for her funeral. I was very close to my grandmother. After that phone call I thought about how much my grandmother had meant to me and how she was largely responsible for who I was, and that's when I wrote my first show, *Stories My Grandmother Told Me*. Many of the stories she told were Anansi tales, and they connected with the stories I was performing at the museum. Suddenly it all made sense. All these things fell into place. Now I always tell stories; my grandmother is my source and I bring her spirit into the room with me wherever I go.

JP: **Since then, you've created numerous solo shows and collaborated with artists from different disciplines and cultures, including Tafelmusik, Canada's internationally acclaimed baroque orchestra.**

EE: Yes, that was for their production of *The Four Seasons*. Never in a million years did I expect something like that to happen. Alison Mackay, one of the orchestra members, wrote a script, then the company hired me to work with them, and there I was thinking, *What do I know about Vivaldi and baroque music?*

JP: **Did the story in the script work for you?**

EE: It was a cute little story about Vivaldi, his children, and a count. I liked the way it was written, but writing and telling, it's not the same. I saw a lot of opportunity for activating the text. So I checked with them and said, "Are you sure you want me to do this? Because I have a certain style."

JP: **(Laughing) You don't stand still and recite a story.**

EE: No, I will *not* stand still and narrate a story. That's not my way. That's not the African way. So they gave me carte blanche to do anything with it. I worked on it and changed the text, and when I read my version for Alison, she was enamored. She said I lifted it off the page. During the performance I changed in and out of character constantly.

JP: **Shapeshifting.**

EE: The production was a wonderful opportunity to showcase African storytelling tradition alongside European baroque music. We also performed with a pipa player (traditional Chinese stringed instrument), a vina player (East Indian stringed instrument), and Inuit throat singers (traditional vocal styling of the northern Inuk). These non-European instruments are much older than the violin or cello, and Inuit throat singing is an ancient tradition. The show brought all of these cultural traditions together, and it worked beautifully.

JP: **How were the other music traditions incorporated?**

EE: All of the music in the show revolved around the four seasons. Seasonal change is something you experience no matter where you live in the world. In the Western world, we have to stop being so Euro-focused. The way we're educating children is so narrow; we should look laterally along the time line.

JP: **Agreed. I have time line books and they're invaluable. One of the books chronicles cultural, scientific, philosophical, and political world events and discoveries from 5000 BC to 2000 AD.**

EE: If we used those books to teach our children, they would have a greater understanding of themselves, different cultures, and the world.

JP: **Speaking of understanding, you have the ability to make movement very accessible for actors and nondancers. I've seen you take novice dancers and turn them into vibrant movers in a couple of weeks. What's your secret?**

EE: I throw different things at them, but first I say, "You cannot have a thought without breath." That's where it starts, with the breath. So we do a lot of breath work and connect our centers to our cores. Everything comes from the center and the center feels it all. When you get nervous, bam! You feel it in your stomach—your center's like a motor. You have to turn it on to get yourself moving. I had a dance teacher in New York who always said, "Dance from your crotch, and if you can't, you might as well put up a sign that says, 'Closed for the season.'"

But basically I tell them dance is about telling stories, and there are many kinds of stories. So when we're warming up, I'll say, "Whatever you've been doing, whatever you were feeling before you came into the studio, use it while you move. Tell me what you're feeling with your movements. Show me what's inside. It doesn't have to make sense to me; it has to make sense to you." And once they get used to this process of energizing their movements with thought and breath, they start communicating. They start telling stories through their dance. Later on we can get technical—polish specific moves and timings. But I start with core work: breath, emotions, stories.

I look at people's eyes. You can't dance with dead eyes. Eyes are so important. You direct your audience with your eyes: Tell them where you want them to look, how you want them to feel, talk to them from heart to heart. With dead eyes there's no engagement. And another thing, and this was told to me by my mentor, Madame Lavinia Williams. Dance is one three-letter word: A-N-D. When we count it's not 1 and 2, and 3 and.... It's 1 *and* 2 *and* 3.... What you do with the *and* is dance. You can teach people technique, do this shape, lift that arm, leap and turn, but there has to be something that puts the technical moves together, and that's the *and*. That's dance. That's each person filling in the space with her own story, her own essence. That's how we make dance speak; that's dance telling stories.

GENERAL ARTS GLOSSARY

This glossary contains brief descriptions of common arts vocabulary used in the text. In keeping with the multidisciplinary nature of the book, the definitions refer to general visual, physical, sonic, emotional, and dramatic aspects of each word. Whenever the word *audience* appears in the definition, it refers to the people viewing and listening to the art.

The classical music terminology used in part II is in a separate glossary following the general arts vocabulary.

action—Something that physically or emotionally moves the performers or audience.

attack—The energy, speed, or pressure behind an action. The method of initiating a sonic, visual, or emotional element.

asymmetry—An individual or group shape that is not the same on both sides (see *symmetry*).

balance—Harmony of sonic, visual, or emotional elements.

beat—A single moment in time or a series of accented sounds, images, or feelings.

color—A distinct sonic, visual, or emotional element that communicates a specific mood or tone. The key is *distinct* which is different from *shade* (see *tone*).

direction—A pathway of movement, sound, or emotion. A place for individuals or a group to face or move away from (see *focus*). Instructions from a choreographer or director.

discord—Clashing or conflicting sonic, visual, or emotional elements.

dynamics—Emotional, sonic, or physical range of a performer. Range of a medium (opacity or transparency) or instrument (volume, pitch, speed).

energy—The physical or emotional content used when performing an action or contained in a piece of sonic, visual, or written art.

focus

external—Direction in which individuals or a group look or move toward. The direction or place that the audience's eye is drawn to.

internal—The level of concentration a person applies to a task.

harmony—When sonic, visual, or emotional elements complement each other.

levels—Heights (high, medium, low) and the increments in between. Application of the heights to create visual shapes, musical chords, emotional complexity, or abstract movement patterns.

line—A series of sounds, images, actions, words, or feelings that may or may not be physically connected but have direction or communicate a specific idea or emotional state.

motif—A sonic, visual, physical, or emotional pattern that is repeated or revisited throughout a piece.

motion—An action that travels through the body. Traveling across the room or performance space. The ebb and flow of sounds, images, and emotions. The action of the audience's eyes while observing the art.

neutral position—Also called parallel position. Spine straight, shoulders over hips, hips over knees, knees over feet, toes facing front, standing hip width apart. Eyes are calm and focused and communicate as little emotion as possible.

pattern—A sonic, visual, physical, or emotional form that may or may not be repeated but is repeatable.

quality—A distinctive sonic, visual, or emotional element.

resonance—Length that a sonic, visual, or emotional element sustains itself in the minds, ears, or eyes of the audience members.

rhythm—A measured flow of sound, visual resonance, or action.

sequence—A running order of movement or sonic-, visual-, or text-based phrases.

shape—Outward form of an object or performer. The sonic form of a sound or composition. The emotional or conceptual form of a dramatic or literary work.

space—The distance between individuals, objects, or notes. The performance area. Negative and positive space are used to describe space when it is full (positive) with an object or sound and space when it is empty (negative).

stage directions—For choreography and blocking purposes, the traditional proscenium stage is divided into the following sections:

downstage—The part of the stage that is closest to the audience.

upstage—The part of the stage that is farthest from the audience.

center stage—The middle part of the stage.

stage right—The area on the right side of the stage (from the dancer's or actor's perspective).

stage left—The area on the left side of the stage (from the dancer's or actor's perspective).

USR	USL	USC
CSR	CSL	CS
DSR	DSL	DSC

symmetry—Individual or group shape, object, image, sonic phrase, or literary work that is the same on both sides, creating a mirror image.

tempo—The speed at which an actions, sounds, or images are presented.

texture—The quality or distinctive feel of a sonic, visual, or emotional element.

time—How people measure existence (past, present, and future). The duration of a solitary action or sound or combination of actions or sounds.

tone—The shade or character of a sonic, visual, or emotional element.

weight—The emotional or physical force used in an action or sound.

MUSIC GLOSSARY

adagio—Played slowly with great expression.

allegro—Played quickly and lively.

bar—Shown in notation as a vertical line through the horizontal staff lines. Each bar contains a set number of beats as determined by the time signature. (The bar can also be called a measure.)

canon (round)—A melody performed when two or more voices sing the same melody one after the other. "Row, Row, Row Your Boat" and "Frère Jacques" are examples of songs sung in canon form.

counterpoint—Melody consisting of two or more voices or lines played simultaneously. Counterpoint works horizontally (imagine two sentences being read across the page at the same time), whereas harmony works vertically (chords are comprised of vertically stacked notes).

gigue—Based on the dance form jig or giga, which is most often played in 6/4 or 6/8 time.

harmony—When notes are played or sung simultaneously to create chords, depth, and richness. Harmony explores the vertical relationship of intervals between notes; counterpoint works horizontally.

largo—Play music broadly and very slowly.

legato—Bound together. The notes flow smoothly together; they are connected with no attack sound to break the stream of sound between notes.

melody—In Greek *melos* means song. A tune in its own right or a theme running through a longer piece of music.

membranephone—A drum constructed by stretching a skin, or membrane, across a frame, or shell.

note—A written symbol used to indicate duration and pitch of a tone by its shape and position on the staff. Notes of a scale are repeated every octave. When a cello and a piccolo play an A, the note is the same but the pitch and tone color are different.

pitch—The frequency of a sound wave. An orchestra, for example, will tune to concert pitch, which is the A above middle C.

staccato—The Italian word meaning detached. Notated by placing a dot under or over the note. The note is played with a clear attack and liftoff.

time signature—Placed at the beginning of a piece of music to show the number of beats (or counts) in a bar (top number) and the type of note being counted per beat (bottom number).

tone color—The quality of the sound of a note. Two instruments might play the same note, but the quality of the note is different.

trill—An ornamentation in which the musician literally shakes the note by quickly playing the notes above or below it within the allotted time value of the note indicated for trilling.

vivace—Played vivaciously; quicker than allegro.

GLOSSARY OF PARTICIPATING ARTISTS

Highlighted Artists

Parmela Attariwala (www.parmela.com)
Emerita Emerencia
Denise Fujiwara (www.fujiwaradance.com)
Ana Francisca de la Mora (www.geocities.com/secondfloorcollective)
Lin Snelling
Nejla Yatkin (www.ny2dance.com)

Photographers

Adam Auer
Antonio Gómez-Palacio
David Hou (www.davidhou.com)
Diana Kolpak (www.torontoclown.com; www.playwrightscanada.com)
John Lauener (www.jlphoto.com)
Avril Patrick (www.avrilpatrick.com)
David Powell (www.puppetmongers.com)
Barry Prophet (www.pomer-prophet.com)
Michael Reinhart (www.quebec-elan.org/showcase/display/portfolio/71; www.myspace/michaelreinhartmusic)
Astrid Rieken
Stefan Rose (www.townsendretraced.ca)

Visual Artist

Shelagh Keeley

ABOUT THE AUTHOR AND THE COMPOSER

Janice Pomer

Janice Pomer has been performing and teaching in the fields of dance, music, and theater since 1976. Her performance work explores the ways in which modern dance can be integrated with other art forms. In 1983, Janice began collaborating with Barry Prophet; together they have created numerous touring productions incorporating modern dance, text, experimental music, found sound, and Barry's kinetic percussion sculptures.

Janice teaches in schools, universities, dance studios, art spaces, and community centers in Canada, offering a variety of movement-based programs and workshops for dancers of all ages and abilities, from beginning youngsters to professional dancers as well as educators. She writes and designs educational programs and dance material for school boards and dance organizations, offering movement education for children and youth. In 2002, Human Kinetics released her first book, *Perpetual Motion: Creative Movement Exercises for Dance and Dramatic Arts*.

Barry Prophet

Barry Prophet is a composer, percussionist, instrument maker, and visual artist who has been creating unique sounds since 1979. His work has appeared in galleries, theaters, and concert halls in Canada, the United States, and Europe. Barry teaches experimental percussion and computer-assisted music programs to learners of all ages and creates sonically charged indoor and outdoor site-specific art.

Janice and Barry live in Toronto, Ontario, Canada. You can learn more about them at www.pomer-prophet.com.

You'll find other outstanding dance resources at
www.HumanKinetics.com

In the U.S. call 1.800.747.4457
Australia 08 8372 0999
Canada. 1.800.465.7301
Europe . . . . .+44 (0) 113 255 5665
New Zealand . . . 0064 9 448 1207

HUMAN KINETICS
The Information Leader in Physical Activity
P.O. Box 5076 • Champaign, IL 61825-5076

MUSIC FINDER

Track	Title	Corresponding exercises	Track length	Notes
1	Slippery Slope	1.1	3:04	Slide whistle. Fun, playful for exploring circular motions.
2	Bent Santoor	1.1	3:15	Atmospheric music sounds like an elastic boomerang.
3	Voices of Air	1.1	3:44	Steady drumming under flute and woodwind sounds.
4	Sputnik	1.2	4:24	Atmospheric, electronic pulses; outer-space and science-fiction feel.
5	Tolling	1.2, 2.2	1:40	Single gong with silence between each beat.
6	Water's Edge	1.3	2:08	Contemplative melody on tubular bells with tabla foundation.
7	Spirit Cave	1.4	2:57	Bowed cymbals over wire drum; mysterious, suspenseful.
8	Li Po	1.5	2:59	Temple block percussion foundation with melodic strings.
9	Saffron Moon	1.6	4:25	Santoor (Asian hammered dulcimer) lyrical solo with variations in tempo and density.
10	Drum Talk	3.1	2:33	Exploration of percussive textures and short rhythmic phrases.
11	Counting	3.2	0:44	Voice counting 5/4 and 7/4.
12	5/4	3.2, 3.3	0:37	8 sets of 1, 2, 3, 1, 2; 8 sets of 1, 2, 1, 2, 1.
13	7/4	3.2	0:50	8 sets of 1, 2, 3, 1, 2, 3, 4; 8 sets of 1, 2, 1, 2, 1, 2, 3.
14	Bell	3.3, 5.3	0:50	Bell sounds every 10 seconds.
15	Water Piano	3.3, 2.2	2:08	Churning, rumbling water with taut wire (tension).
16	Mountain Pass	3.3, 2.2	2:58	Gentle, rhythmic gongs.
17	Jazz Modern Tempo	3.4	1:55	Composition for jazz trio in moderate time.
18	Jazz Slow Tempo	3.4	2:17	Same piece as track 17 but slower.
19	Jazz Fast Tempo	3.4	1:32	Same piece as track 17 but faster.
20	Polished	4.1, 1.4	1:32	Bowed glass, crystalline.
21	Rough	4.1	1:33	Snake drain, drilling, coarse.
22	Bubble	4.1	1:32	Slide whistle in solo and duet.
23	Tone, Pitch, Color A	4.2	0:57	Same note and pitch but different tone color.
24	Tone, Pitch, Color B	4.2	0:59	Same note and tone color but different pitch.

Track	Title	Corresponding exercises	Track length	Notes
25	Tone, Pitch, Color C	4.2	1:01	Same note, different tone color and pitch.
26	Media Play	4.4	2:09	Layered and looped voices from media broadcasts with additional sonic textures.
27	Pace With Worry	5.1	1:02	Footsteps with crunch and rumble.
28	Stammer With Indecision	5.1	1:02	Clusters of electronic pulses going on and off.
29	Nerves Shatter	5.1	1:03	Drilling with bamboo clatter.
30	Bubble With Excitement	5.1	1:02	Tongue drum: fast mallet work with warm resonance.
31	Squirm With Embarrassment	5.1	1:02	Mono bend: bending a wire to make it talk.
32	Float With Happiness	5.1	1:02	Mallet on metal bells.
33	Shake With Glee	5.1	1:04	Laughter manipulated.
34	Vowel Vocal	6.2	2:08	Vocal exploration of *a, e, i, o, u.*
35	Chinese Crash	Culminating Exercise for Dance and Music	0:06	Sound library.
36	Gong	Culminating Exercise for Dance and Music	0:11	Sound library.
37	Ride Cymbal Bell	Culminating Exercise for Dance and Music	0:07	Sound library.
38	Ride Cymbal	Culminating Exercise for Dance and Music	0:06	Sound library.
39	Splash Cymbal	Culminating Exercise for Dance and Music	0:06	Sound library.
40	Bass Drum Vintage	Culminating Exercise for Dance and Music	0:06	Sound library.
41	Snare Heavy	Culminating Exercise for Dance and Music	0:06	Sound library.

(continued)

(continued)

Track	Title	Corresponding exercises	Track length	Notes
42	Tom Floor	Culminating Exercise for Dance and Music	0:06	Sound library.
43	Tom High	Culminating Exercise for Dance and Music	0:06	Sound library.
44	Tom Mid	Culminating Exercise for Dance and Music	0:06	Sound library.
45	Darbuka Phrase	Culminating Exercise for Dance and Music	0:11	Sound library.
46	Double Udu Sequence	Culminating Exercise for Dance and Music	0:14	Sound library.
47	Frame Drum Phrase	Culminating Exercise for Dance and Music	0:06	Sound library.
48	Japanese Tubular Bells	Culminating Exercise for Dance and Music	0:18	Sound library.
49	Junkbau Sequence	Culminating Exercise for Dance and Music	0:07	Sound library.
50	Percussion 1	Culminating Exercise for Dance and Music	0:07	Sound library.
51	Santoor 3	Culminating Exercise for Dance and Music	0:07	Sound library.
52	Santoor Minor 1	Culminating Exercise for Dance and Music	0:21	Sound library.
53	Santoor Minor 2	Culminating Exercise for Dance and Music	0:11	Sound library.

Track	Title	Corresponding exercises	Track length	Notes
54	Java 1	Culminating Exercise for Dance and Music	0:06	Sound library.
55	Java 2	Culminating Exercise for Dance and Music	0:06	Sound library.
56	Java 3	Culminating Exercise for Dance and Music	0:06	Sound library.
57	Java 4	Culminating Exercise for Dance and Music	0:06	Sound library.
58	Java 5	Culminating Exercise for Dance and Music	0:06	Sound library.
59	Java Roll 1	Culminating Exercise for Dance and Music	0:06	Sound library.
60	Java Roll 2	Culminating Exercise for Dance and Music	0:06	Sound library.
61	Java Roll 3	Culminating Exercise for Dance and Music	0:06	Sound library.
62	Java Roll 4	Culminating Exercise for Dance and Music	0:06	Sound library.
63	Java Roll 5	Culminating Exercise for Dance and Music	0:06	Sound library.
64	Four Footsteps on Gravel	Culminating Exercise for Dance and Music	0:06	Sound library.
65	Bottle Soccer Clip	Culminating Exercise for Dance and Music	0:06	Sound library.

(continued)

Track	Title	Corresponding exercises	Track length	Notes
66	Crash Carts Clip	Culminating Exercise for Dance and Music	0:06	Sound library.
67	Drops on Pipe	Culminating Exercise for Dance and Music	0:13	Sound library.
68	Factory Press	Culminating Exercise for Dance and Music	0:32	Sound library.
69	Pully Track Clip	Culminating Exercise for Dance and Music	0:06	Sound library.
70	Rain	Culminating Exercise for Dance and Music	0:20	Sound library.
71	Wire Res 2	Culminating Exercise for Dance and Music	0:16	Sound library.
72	Wire Res	Culminating Exercise for Dance and Music	0:14	Sound library.
73	Prophet Example	Culminating Exercise for Dance and Music	0:38	Recreate this track to become familiar with the Audacity software and the sound library.

Precise track times may vary depending on the software being used.